ON THE HIGHWAY

The Bible For The Children, From Genesis To Revelation. Illustrated By Object - Lessons, Chalk-Talks, Sand-Board, And Stories For The Use Of Junior Workers, Primary Teachers, And Mothers. Also For Supplementary Work.

By Ella N. Wood

Author of "Chalk," "Object - Lessons For Junior Work," etc.

First Fruits Press
Wilmore, Kentucky
c2015

On the highway: the Bible for the children, from Genesis to Revelation, by Ella N. Wood.

First Fruits Press, ©2015
Previously published: Boston and Chicago: United Society of Christian Endeavor, ©1921.

ISBN: 9781621714095 (print), 9781621714101 (digital)

Digital version at http://place.asburyseminary.edu/christianendeavorbooks/27/

First Fruits Press is a digital imprint of the Asbury Theological Seminary, B.L. Fisher Library. Asbury Theological Seminary is the legal owner of the material previously published by the Pentecostal Publishing Co. and reserves the right to release new editions of this material as well as new material produced by Asbury Theological Seminary. Its publications are available for noncommercial and educational uses, such as research, teaching and private study. First Fruits Press has licensed the digital version of this work under the Creative Commons Attribution Noncommercial 3.0 United States License. To view a copy of this license, visit http://creativecommons.org/licenses/by-nc/3.0/us/.

For all other uses, contact:

First Fruits Press
B.L. Fisher Library
Asbury Theological Seminary
204 N. Lexington Ave.
Wilmore, KY 40390
http://place.asburyseminary.edu/firstfruits

Wood, Ella Nancy, 1862-
   On the highway: the Bible for the children, from Genesis to Revelation / by Ella N. Wood.
   ix, 188 pages ; 21 cm.
   Wilmore, Ky. : First Fruits Press, ©2015.
   Reprint. Previously published: Boston: United Society of Christian Endeavor, ©1921.
   ISBN: 9781621714095 (pbk.)
   1. Bible – Study and teaching. 2. Object-teaching. 3. Chalk-talks. I. Title.
BS605 .W6 2015

Cover design by Jonathan Ramsay

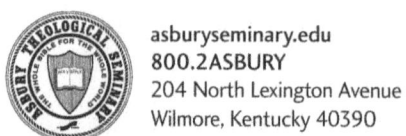

asburyseminary.edu
800.2ASBURY
204 North Lexington Avenue
Wilmore, Kentucky 40390

First Fruits Press
The Academic Open Press of Asbury Theological Seminary
204 N. Lexington Ave., Wilmore, KY 40390
859-858-2236
first.fruits@asburyseminary.edu
asbury.to/firstfruits

ON THE HIGHWAY

ON THE HIGHWAY

THE BIBLE FOR THE CHILDREN, FROM GENESIS TO REVELATION. ILLUSTRATED BY OBJECT-LESSONS, CHALK-TALKS, SAND-BOARD, AND STORIES FOR THE USE OF JUNIOR WORKERS, PRIMARY TEACHERS, AND MOTHERS. ALSO FOR SUPPLEMENTARY WORK.

BY

ELLA N. WOOD

AUTHOR OF "CHALK," "OBJECT-LESSONS FOR JUNIOR WORK," ETC.

"And a highway shall be there, and a way, and it shall be called the way of holiness."

UNITED SOCIETY OF CHRISTIAN ENDEAVOR
BOSTON   CHICAGO

COPYRIGHTED, 1921, BY THE
UNITED SOCIETY OF CHRISTIAN ENDEAVOR

INTRODUCTION

"And behold there was a very stately palace before him, the name of which was Beautiful; and it stood by the highway-side."

The feet are very small when they start out on the highway towards the Palace Beautiful, and need the guidance of those who have travelled far. Let us take care that before they meet their Apollyon they will be walking side by side with the Master.

It has been my endeavor, through picture and story, to make the people they meet "on the highway" so real, God so loving, and Christ so helpful, that the study of the Bible will become a joy.

In planning this book it has been my thought that to study it lesson by lesson would not only give the child a comprehensive view of the Bible, but bring clearly before his mind in a simplified manner its vital truths.

Many of these lessons were published in "Junior Topics Outlined," which is now out of print; but they have been worked over, and, I trust made better and more adaptable to all grades.

ELLA N. WOOD

EAST LANSING, MICH.

CONTENTS

	PAGE
INTRODUCTION	v

PART I
OLD TESTAMENT STORIES

THE BIBLE	3
GOD OUR CREATOR	5
GOD'S LOVING CARE	8
A JOURNEY TO CANAAN	10
HOW GOD SAVED A BOY	12
THE STORY OF A BOY AND HIS FATHER	14
A BAD BARGAIN	16
THE FIRST TITHE	18
A CHANGED NAME	20
JOSEPH: HIS GREAT TRIAL	22
JOSEPH RETURNS GOOD FOR EVIL	24
A LITTLE BASKET	26
GOD'S HOLY PLACES	29
AN UNWILLING SERVANT	31
GRUMBLING	34
THE SABBATH COMMANDMENT	36
THOU SHALT NOTS	37
MAN'S FAITH AND GOD'S PROMISE	38
GIANTS AND GRASSHOPPERS	40
A CORD OF BLUE	42
SERPENTS	44
AN ANIMAL THAT TALKED	47
A MAN OF COURAGE	49
A CORD OF RED	51
COURAGE, AND A BIG NOISE	53

CONTENTS

Gideon and His Brave Men	56
Samson	58
Ruth, a Loving Daughter	60
A Boy Who Worked for God	62
A Little Messenger	64
A King God Chose	66
A Prince Who was True	68
God's Test	70
A Boy and a Giant	72
A Royal Friendship	74
A Gift that God Likes	77
The Lord's House	79
God's Birds	82
An Unhappy King	84
Perseverance	86
The Brave Queen	88
Mordecai the Faithful	90
The Bible-lover's Psalm	91
The Twenty-third Psalm	93
A Psalm of Praise	95
A Lesson from the Longest Psalm	97
Trust	98
Our Words	100
Known by Our Deeds	103
Remember Thy Creator	105
The Little Foxes	106
God's Prophets and Their Message	107
Isaiah Tells about Christ	109
The Sabbath: How Make It a Day of Delight	111
Called of God: Jeremiah, Ourselves	113
Our Common Blessings	115
How to Get a New Heart	117
How One Boy Showed His Colors	118
A Lions' Den	120
Short-lived Goodness	122

CONTENTS

A Boy who Shirked..................................	124
The Last Journey in the Old Testament...........	125

PART II

NEW TESTAMENT STORIES

What the Wise Men Found.......................	129
The Boy Jesus.....................................	131
Christ Choosing His Helpers.....................	133
A Beautiful Well..................................	135
Christ and the Nobleman's Son...................	138
Christ's Beatitudes...............................	140
"A Shine-out" Lesson.............................	142
The Kind of Praying Jesus Likes.................	144
The Sabbath Day...................................	146
Four Kinds of People..............................	147
Jesus Feeds the Hungry...........................	148
A Lesson in Forgiveness..........................	150
Jesus in Our Homes...............................	152
Our Neighbors.....................................	154
Jesus, the Good Shepherd.........................	157
The Children's Hosannas..........................	159
The Greatest Commandment.........................	161
Our Talents.......................................	163
Spring Flowers and the Risen Christ..............	167
A Shipwreck.......................................	170
How Christ Wants Us to Care for Our Bodies....	172
Talking to God....................................	174
Making the Best of Things........................	177
How to Keep Sweet.................................	179
A Missionary Lesson...............................	181
What Jesus Bore for Us...........................	183
Vanity Fair.......................................	185
Heaven	187

PART ONE
OLD TESTAMENT STORIES

ON THE HIGHWAY

OUR BIBLE
(JOHN 5: 39)

Prepare an object-lesson as follows:

Cut a cross, a heart, an anchor, a crown, and a torch out of white cardboard. These should be about four inches long and wide in proportion. On the cross print the reference Luke 9: 23; on the anchor, 1 Tim. 6: 12; on the heart, Matt. 5: 8; on the crown, 1 Pet. 5: 4; on the torch, Prov. 5: 1.

Cut from a magazine the picture of a house or "mansion." Mount this on cardboard, and print under it the reference John 14: 2. Cover a square board or heavy pasteboard with black, and tack these objects on it; put a string in the top corner of the board by which to hang it on the wall. If this is made with care, it will be a very pretty wall-piece, and can be left on the wall throughout the year.

At the previous lesson ask the pupils to bring their Bibles. After the topic is announced and the

Scripture read ask the pupils to rise, fall into line, and march to an appropriate song, forming a circle around the table. Let each pupil lay his Bible on the table; then ask that all heads be bowed and that the pupils ask God to help them to love their Bible and obey its commands. The pupils will again march to the table, take their Bibles, and go to their seats.

Have the pupils turn to the reference on the cross and read it in concert. By a few careful questions draw from them what it stands for, what it means to "follow Christ." Also lead them to tell you all they can about the cross and its relation to us. Proceed in this way with each object, being careful to draw from the pupils the lesson the Bible gives us regarding it. If there is time, close with a short Bible drill, such as naming the books of the Bible. This can be done in different ways. One way would be to divide the class into sides. Let one side name all the books in the Old Testament they can remember, and the other side the books of the New Testament. Another way is to give each child one or two letters of the alphabet and let him name the books beginning with his letter.

GOD OUR CREATOR
(GEN. 1: 1-31)

We will illustrate this lesson by combining a chalk-talk and a sand-board object-lesson. The materials needed will be, blackboard and chalk, a sand-board (if you have none, make one by tacking some yardsticks or other narrow strips around a bread-board or small table), some moist sand, small stones, moss or turf, some small branches of trees, flowers, a small pail of water, a cup or shallow dish, a yard of light-blue cheese-cloth, and some stars and a moon cut from silver or white paper. Your boys will furnish you with sand, branches, etc.; and the girls will prepare stars, etc. The more you let the children help you, the more interested they will become.

The purpose of this lesson is to give the pupils an idea of God's great goodness and wisdom in planning the world.

First write on the blackboard the words "In the beginning was God." After the words draw a brace, and let the pupils suggest the different names that have been applied to God; as they are named, write them in the brace. It will work out something like this:

IN THE BEGINNING WAS GOD $\begin{cases} \text{CREATOR} \\ \text{LORD} \\ \text{JEHOVAH} \\ \text{FATHER} \\ \text{FRIEND} \\ \text{etc.} \end{cases}$

If you have the time, the blackboard lesson may be carried out farther by writing questions as follows:

What is God?

Where is God?

What did God make?

What was God's greatest work?

How does God take care of the things He has made?

A brace may be drawn after each question and filled by answers suggested by the pupils.

Have the sand placed on the sand-board in an irregular pile. This will represent the earth as "waste and void" (let the Bible verses be read carefully); tell the story of creation; or, better still, draw it from the pupils. Show the water; and, as you talk or question, let the sand be spread on the board, forming hills, mountains, valleys. Sink the cup, and fill it with water to represent a lake. If you can secure a piece of mirror, lay it in the sand and form a river; then, as your story grows, plant the trees and flowers. If some little Noah's-ark animals and people can be provided, the story can be carried out to the creation of animal life and man. At just the right time have the cheese-cloth stretched over the board about two feet above, the moon and stars having been previously arranged upon it. This represents the heavens.

Place special emphasis on the fact that God created all these things out of nothing; and this shows His infinite wisdom and wonderful power. No one but God could do this. We can make things, but we cannot create things.

Make clear to your class that the last and best thing that God created was *man*, and that He made man in His own image. Lead the pupils to talk of the wonderful way in which they are made. Let them examine their hands, and study them; also the eye, etc. This lesson may be enlarged on as much as the teacher sees fit.

GOD'S LOVING CARE
(Gen. 8: 1-4, 15-20)

For an object-lesson cut a cross out of white blotting-paper. It should be just large enough to stand upright in an ordinary plain glass tumbler. Saturate it with red ink or Diamond dye. Take this and a glass tumbler to the meeting.

Make a large brace on the blackboard, and in front of it write the words "How God saves." Show a glass of water. Lead the pupils to tell of some of the uses of water, also of its destructive power. Mention the St. Louis flood, the rapid rivers after the heavy rains, etc.

Speak of how many a drink of water has saved a life. Then lead the thought to how God saved Noah from the water. Have one of the pupils fill the brace with words suggested by the pupils as they name ways in which God cares for people and saves them.

Ask the pupils to name the greatest and best thing God ever did to save His people. Show the red cross. They will at once name Jesus. Ask them to repeat John 3: 16 in concert.

Hold up the glass of water. We will call that "our lives." Place the cross in the glass. The effect will be almost magical. The water will at once take a bright red color with the cross showing through. The lesson is easily drawn that, when we take God's gifts into our lives, they are at once made beautiful, through and through, by the blood of Jesus Christ. Ask that all heads be bowed and each pupil ask that God will save him and help him to love Jesus.

A JOURNEY TO CANAAN
(Gen. 12: 6-9; 13: 1-5)

To-day we have the story of Abraham as he went on his journey to Canaan as God had told him to do. One thought to impress is that he took God with him.

When we go on a journey, we take everything with us we think we shall need — a clothes-brush, to keep our clothes clean; a tooth-brush that we may keep our teeth clean; comb and brush, etc. These are all right, and we should never forget to take such things with us; but, when we pack our satchels, we should not forget to put in the one thing that will help us to keep our hearts clean. The pupils will tell you that this one thing is our Bible. Abraham did not have any Bible to take, but he stopped right in the middle of his journey. (Draw a large tree with a man under it and a tent near by.) Lead the pupils to tell the story from this point. (Draw an altar.) Also lead the pupils to see that we do not have to build an altar in order to honor God. Then ask how we can honor God.

Outline a small church on the blackboard; make a brace in front of it; ask the pupils to fill the brace with ways in which we may honor God in church. Draw a schoolhouse, playground, home, etc., and treat them as above described.

HOW GOD SAVED A BOY
(GEN. 21: 14-20)

Once upon a time there were two little boys. (Draw some figures on the blackboard to represent two boys.) One of them was named Isaac; the other, Ishmael. (Write the names over the boys.) Isaac was the son of Sarah, Abraham's wife; and Ishmael was the son of Hagar, a bondwoman. Sarah did not like Hagar very well; so she told Abraham to send Hagar and Ishmael away. So one day Hagar took her little boy and a bottle of water, and wandered away into the wilderness. (Draw some trees and figures to represent Hagar and Ishmael.)

Now, Hagar thought she did not have a friend in all the world. She was very lonely, and her heart was sad. She did not know what would become of her little boy. After a while all the water in the bottle was gone, and there was no water to be had in the wilderness. She knew her boy must die, and with her heart breaking she laid him under a shady tree (draw a small tree with the boy lying under it), and went away so that

OLD TESTAMENT STORIES 13

she might not see him suffer and die. She sat down and cried.

This poor, heartbroken woman was not alone. "God heard the voice of the lad," and sent an angel out of heaven to comfort her. (Write the word "God" on the blackboard, and outline two wings to represent the angel. Ask the pupils to name other incidents where God sent an angel.) The angel told Hagar to go and get her little boy and hold him, for he would make a great nation. Then Hagar opened her eyes, and saw before her a well of water. (Draw a well.) O joy! now her boy could live. She hastened to the well, and filled the bottle, and gave the poor suffering boy a drink. "And God was with the lad; and he grew, and dwelt in the wilderness, and became an archer." (Draw the boy with a bow and arrow.)

The story will be much more interesting if instead of being told or read it is drawn from the pupils. As they tell the story, guided by yourself, sketch the pictures.

The lesson to impress is that God cares for us and will always provide for us.

THE STORY OF A BRAVE BOY AND HIS FATHER

(GEN. 22: 1-14; HEB. 11: 17, 18)

Arrange with your sunshine committee or class to meet at your home on Saturday afternoon and bring with them all the cut flowers they can secure.

Prepare a number of slips of paper with texts about faith written on them. The slips should be about an inch wide and six inches long. Tie a bit of sand-silk thread in one end of each, and fold them as small as possible.

Have the flowers made up into little bouquets, and tie one of the slips in the centre of each.

Have your sand-board prepared with moist sand. Scoop out the sand in the shape of a hollow anchor; place the little bouquets in the groove and press the sand about them. Outline the word "Faith" beneath the anchor with pansies or other small flowers.

Have the lesson story told by the pupils. Write the words "Obedience" and "Faith" on the blackboard. Impress the lesson of faith in God.

Have the pupils come forward, one at a time,

OLD TESTAMENT STORIES 15

take a bunch of flowers from the sand-board, read the slip, and place the flowers in a basket. Have each text discussed after it is read.

The flowers may be taken to the hospital or to the sick and shut-in by a committee of the pupils. The following texts may be used on the slips.

Heb. 6: 19.	John 20: 29.	Gal. 3: 22.
Matt. 8: 13.	Heb. 10: 22.	Prov. 28: 25.
Mark 9: 23.	Heb. 12: 2.	Prov. 29: 25.
Mark 11: 24.	1 John 3: 23.	Prov. 30: 5.
Luke 17: 6.	1 John 5: 14.	Ps. 55: 22.
John 14: 1.	Rev. 3: 20.	Ps. 40: 4.
John 14: 12.	Acts 10: 43.	Ps. 37: 3–7.
John 20: 27.		

A BAD BARGAIN
(GEN. 25: 27–34; PHIL. 4: 8)

Make a heart of white cardboard or heavy paper. It should be about six inches across. Print on it the words "Our Birthright." Take the following objects to the meeting: Some vegetables in a dish (these may be made red by putting in with them pieces of a beet), a bottle half full of cold tea, a playing-card, a fashion-book, a cigarette, and a yellow-backed novel.

First of all make clear to the pupils what Esau's birthright was.

The first-born among the Jews enjoyed special privileges among his brethren. Among these were a special consecration to the Lord to serve as a priest, greater dignity, a double portion of his father's estate, and authority in his father's absence.

Follow this with the thought of our birthright. Have one of the pupils read Gen. 1: 27, and another one, John 1: 12. Show the white heart, and lead the pupils to see that God gives every boy and girl this birthright.

Show the dish of vegetables. This represents the

"mess of pottage" that Esau took for his birthright. In a moment of physical weakness and temptation he sold the best thing he had for a dish of food that he could eat in a few minutes. Then lead the thought to ways in which people sell their birthrights. Show the bottle which represents liquor, the playing-card, the cigarette, the fashion-book, etc. People sell their birthrights for a glass of beer, a game of cards, a cigarette. Women sell their souls for fashion, and men and women often barter their birthrights for a dance or an hour's pleasure. A boy often bargains with Satan in a game for keeps, for it is the first step in gambling.

Ask the pupils what we can put in the place of these things. Have the second reference of the lesson read, and lead the pupils to discuss each virtue mentioned.

Show a Bible, and tell the pupils that there is a book called the New Testament, which tells us how to take care of our birthright. Lead them to recall some of Christ's teachings in His Sermon on the Mount, Matt. 5-7.

Close with a prayer service in which the pupils will ask God to help them to value their birthrights above everything.

THE FIRST TITHE
(GEN. 28: 12-22)

Illustrate the one-tenth by showing ten dimes. One of them is a tenth. If we had but a dollar, and wanted to give a tithe to the Lord, we should give ten cents. If we had ten cents, one cent would be our tithe.

Make clear to the pupils that if they have a regular income, if they sell papers, or if mother pays them for errands, if father gives them a certain sum of money each week for their own, and they want to give a tenth of it to the Lord, they must divide the amount by ten, and the quotient will be their tithe. If it seems wise at this time, lead your pupils to become members of the Tenth Legion. By sending to the United Society of Christian Endeavor, 41 Mt. Vernon Street, Boston, Mass., you can secure literature on this subject.

Tithing-crosses, holding ten dimes, can be had by sending to the Christian Finance Association, New York, N. Y. A postal card to this address will secure you a catalogue of these.

The lesson that money is not the only thing we

OLD TESTAMENT STORIES 19

can give the Lord should be made very clear. We should give of our substance to those who are needy; we should give our sympathy to the lame and afflicted. There are a hundred things we can give in the way of help and service.

The following references may be used as a Bible reading on the topic:

1 Chron. 29:5.	Acts 20:35.
Prov. 11:24, 25.	Rom. 12:8.
Prov. 21:26.	2 Cor. 9:6.
Prov. 22:9.	1 Tim. 6:18, 19.
Eccl. 11:1.	2 Cor. 8:7.
Luke 6:38.	2 Cor. 8:11.

Teach Matt. 25:40 as a memory verse.

A CHANGED NAME
(Gen. 32:22-32)

Jacob wrestled in his own strength till he became disabled; then he saw how weak he was.

He would not let go till the Lord had blessed him.

We should hang on to God, and the blessing will come to us just as surely as it did to Jacob.

If we wrestle long enough with our difficulties, God will in the end bless us.

Jacob was alone with God when the blessing came. We should seek to be alone with God when we need His special blessing and help. Jacob saw God face to face. If we would see God face to face, we must wrestle with sin till we overcome; then we can hear the voice of Jesus say, "Well done, thou good servant; because thou wast found faithful in a very little, have thou authority over ten cities."

The Ant and the King

Once there was a king who was very unhappy. He had been defeated on every hand. His armies had been overcome and his kingdom overthrown.

He sat one day in a cave where he was hiding from his enemies. Sad and discouraged, defeated and deserted, he thought he might as well stay there and starve to death.

As he sat there, he spied an ant crawling up the wall of the cave. The ant was carrying a fly twice as large as himself. He climbed up a few feet, and fell back to the floor. He started up again. This time he climbed a little higher, then fell to the floor again. The king thought, "Surely he will not try it again"; but the ant, apparently not the least discouraged, climbed again, but, alas! fell. Six times did the little ant with his heavy load try to climb to the top of the cave, but fell every time. The king became interested in such splendid courage, and with joy he saw the ant reach his goal after trying seven times. He jumped up and said, "I will learn a lesson from this little ant. I will go and fight till I conquer, and regain my kingdom."

The old Norman king was as good as his word.

Let the prayers be for strength to persevere in our fight with our besetting sins.

JOSEPH: HIS GREAT TRIAL

(GEN. 37: 23-28)

Two or three weeks previous to this time get cheap pictures bearing on the life of Joseph. If you can afford to get enough to present to the pupils, all the better.

Have one of the girls make a little coat of cloth of several bright colors, and line it with bright red cambric. Pin this near the centre of the top of the blackboard. We will go back a little and show what led Joseph's brothers to treat him as they did. Directly under the coat draw a figure to represent a sheaf of wheat, and in a semicircle around this draw some figures to represent sheaves bowing toward the one in the centre.

Draw some braces on the blackboard, and have the pupils suggest words to fill them. The following are suggestive.

THE BROTHERS
- Envious
- Cruel
- Wicked
- Deceitful
- Murderous
- Hated Joseph
- Selfish
- Liars

JOSEPH
- Innocent
- God's servant
- Helpless
- Honest

OLD TESTAMENT STORIES 23

Make the lesson bear strongly on these points, especially the sin of envy and deception. Ask the pupils to name some of the qualities the brothers lacked.

Lacked $\begin{cases} \text{Love} \\ \text{Trust} \\ \text{Good will} \\ \text{True hearts} \\ \text{Honesty} \end{cases}$

Whose example may we follow that will give us these qualities? Outline a cross on the blackboard, and by a few earnest words lead the pupils to feel the constant need of Christ in the life to help us keep from being like Joseph's brothers.

JOSEPH RETURNS GOOD FOR EVIL
(Gen. 45:4-11)

For the object-lesson make a small bag about five inches wide and nine inches long; fill this two-thirds full of wheat or other grain. Have a small silver cup (a tin cup will answer) and some silver money.

Draw a heart on the blackboard, and write the words "Joseph's life" in it. Around it make some arrows with the points toward the heart.

Lead the pupils to tell the story of Joseph and his brethren. Go still farther back, and have the pupils name all the wrong things that Joseph's brothers had done to him. As they are named, write them on the arrows. Make the lesson clear that these wrong acts had pierced Joseph's heart like arrows, and that Joseph had much to forgive. Ask of whom this reminds them. Draw a cross on the blackboard. Ask one of the pupils to read Matt. 18:21, 22. Multiply seventy by seven, and make the lesson clear that Christ meant that we should keep on forgiving, no matter how often any one wrongs us; that this is the Christ-like spirit of forgiving.

OLD TESTAMENT STORIES

Have one of the pupils prepared to come forward with the little bag of grain and tell how Joseph not only forgave his brothers, but gave them an abundance of food, all they could carry, and put the money they had given him in pay in the bags of wheat, and how in Benjamin's bag he put a silver cup.

Here let the pupils put the money into the bag and tie it up. Hang the bag beside the little "coat of many colors."

Make the teaching clear that God not only forgives us if we ask Him, but gives us an abundance of good things all the time. Have the pupils name some of the good things God gives us.

Make the application of the lesson personal, and teach Matt. 6: 14, 15.

Close with a prayer service, and suggest that all ask God to help them to forgive freely and fully.

A LITTLE BASKET
(Exod. 2: 1-10)

The material for the object-lesson will consist of a candle (a small Christmas candle will be best), some slips of writing-paper an inch and a half long and a quarter of an inch wide, a bottle with a mouth large enough to hold the candle, and about three inches high, and some crêpe tissue-paper. Tinfoil or other decorative paper may be substituted.

Place the candle in the bottle for a candlestick. Cut the paper six inches wide and from fifteen to eighteen inches long. Gather this on one side about an inch and a half from the top, and tie it around the neck of the bottle. Three inches below this tie it around the base of the bottle. Spread out the lower edge of the paper for the bowl of the candlestick.

Write words on the slips of paper suggestive of the different things that make up a life, such as "Love," "Play," "Work," "Study," "Happiness," "Smiles," "Jesus," etc. Paste these at intervals around the candle.

OLD TESTAMENT STORIES 27

Before beginning the life of Moses and his leadership of the Israelites get pictures bearing on these lessons.

Draw the lesson story from the pupils. Children are always charmed with this thrilling event, and will picture the scene most vividly.

To-day our lesson is to be about the beginning of a life which was great with service. Show the candle, and light it. Show how this represents a life just beginning to shine for Jesus. Impress the thought that God has a plan for every life. He will make each one of us as useful in the world as He made Moses, if we will let Him. Sometimes we spoil God's plans for ourselves by being disobedient and wilful, just as we could spoil the little candle so that it would be of no use to any one.

Read the words on the slips about the candle; have them discussed one by one. After this have the pupils form a circle about the candle and sing softly, "Lead, kindly Light." If you have the book called "Chalk," illustrate the song on the blackboard as suggested there.

"Jesus bids us shine
With a clear, pure light
Like a little candle,
Burning in the night.

*" In the world is darkness,
So we must shine,
You in your small corner,
And I in mine."*

Another poem that might be used is the following:

*"Little words are sometimes mighty;
Little lights shine far away;
So, then, we will shine for Jesus,
Shine for Jesus every day.*

*"Shine out for Jesus!
Let each little candle shine;
He will guide and safely shelter
Us with arms divine."*

GOD'S HOLY PLACES
(Exod. 3: 5)

For the object-lesson have a picture of Christ, the picture of a church, and a branch of red autumn leaves. If the leaves cannot be had, a leafless branch may be supplied with red tissue-paper leaves pasted or wired on.

The meaning of the word "reverence" may be made clear to the pupils by using an illustration somewhat like the following:

Suppose we had a friend who had been very good to us, and every time we went to see him we should smoke a pipe, and spit around the floor, and talk loudly and coarsely, laugh in his face, make fun of what he said, and use his name in a disrespectful manner; do you think we should be showing reverence and respect for him?

Lead the pupils to tell what would be showing reverence to such a friend.

Have one of the pupils tell the story of the burning bush. She may show the branch with the red leaves. She should dwell particularly on the voice.

Liken the burning bush to nature, and show that God speaks to us with a still small voice out of the flowers and trees and grass. His loving-kindness and constant care are all around us in His beautiful handiwork. Ask the pupils whether they have not seen such wonderful scenes in nature that they felt a kind of reverence, and, as we often say, like taking off their hats.

Lead the thought along the line of reverence to God and God's house. Show the pictures. Try to impress the sacredness of the church. Have the pupils tell how we can reverence God's house, and how we sometimes act irreverently in church. Make a list of each of these ways on the blackboard.

Show how Joseph reverenced his father. He reverenced and honored him because he loved him. If we love God, we shall reverence Him.

AN UNWILLING SERVANT
(EXOD. 3: 10-14; 4: 10-12)

A pretty gift to accompany this lesson will be some little canes or staves cut from colored cardboard. These should be six or eight inches long and have a crook at one end. Cut one just the size and shape you want, and use it for a pattern by laying it on the sheet of cardboard and marking around it with a pencil. Have some of your pupils cut them out. On the side of each cane print a Bible reference to one of God's promises of help. The list given below may be used. Tie a knot of baby ribbon on one end of each cane and they are complete.

Isa. 32: 20.	Luke 12: 42, 43.	1 Tim. 6: 20.
Jer. 1: 8.	1 Tim. 1: 18.	2 Tim. 1: 13.
Matt. 10: 16.	1 Tim. 4: 15.	2 Tim. 2: 1.
Matt. 28: 19.	1 Tim. 4: 16.	2 Tim. 2: 3.
Mark 16: 15.	1 Tim. 6: 11.	2 Tim. 3: 14.
Matt. 10: 28.	1 Tim. 6: 14.	2 Tim. 4: 5.

Ask one of the older pupils to meet with you before the meeting and talk over the Scripture lesson, including the first seventeen verses of the fourth chapter of Exodus. This will give the lesson of God's help to Moses, His promise to be with him, to put words into his mouth, etc. Then at the meeting ask this pupil to tell the lesson story.

Ask the pupils to name other Bible men who did not want to do what God asked them to. They may mention "Jonah," the "rich young man," etc.

Did we ever refuse or fail to do what we knew God would like to have us do?

How do we know that God wants us to do certain things? These questions will lead to a general discussion of the lesson.

Have the gifts passed among the pupils. Just as Moses was to take his staff as a reminder of God's promise to be with him, so these little staves are to be reminders of God's promise to help us. Ask each pupil to find his reference in the Bible. Then ask each one to rise, read his verse, and add a word of testimony.

A very pretty and simple exercise would be to have the song "I'll Go Where You Want Me to Go" acted out by three of the pupils. The song is found in the "Endeavor Hymnal" published by the United Society of Christian Endeavor, 41 Mt. Vernon Street, Boston, Mass.

This should be arranged for and planned previous to the meeting. Have the first verse illustrated with pictures, the first line by a picture of mountains and water, the second line by the picture of a battle. Have the third line sung softly, and the pupil will raise his hand while singing the last line.

The second verse may be illustrated by the singer's showing an illuminated text, or one printed in large letters on cardboard, for the first line of the song, the picture of the prodigal son or some other similar character for the second line; then with clasped hands and closed eyes sing the two remaining lines as a prayer.

The first line of the third verse may be illustrated by a picture of the world or a globe, the second line by a small cross, the fourth line by a cardboard text. With a little practice three singers can give this exercise in a most pleasing manner.

Have the three come forward and stand behind a table on which objects are laid in the order in which they are to be used. Let each one sing his verse alone and all the pupils join in the chorus.

Follow this with a service of sentence prayers.

GRUMBLING
(Exod. 16: 1-7)

The following braces, if carefully and fully worked out, will fill the lesson hour. Have the words which fill the braces suggested by the pupils, and discuss each after it is written in the brace. Show how grumbling about God, clothes, etc., is really finding fault with God.

What were the Israelites grumbling about? { They were dissatisfied with { Their food, Moses, Aaron } God }

What do we grumble about? { Our food, Our clothes, Our friends, Our homes, Our lessons, The weather, etc. } God

How did God try to please these people?

Have one of the pupils tell the story of the lesson.

For what may we trust God?
{ Food
Clothes
Home
Friends
Sunshine
Flowers
Happiness
Eternal life
etc. }

In what particular things should we obey God?
{ Loyalty
Love
Service
Prayer
Faith
etc. }

THE SABBATH COMMANDMENT
(Exod. 20: 8-11)

Write Exod. 20:8 on the blackboard. Under this draw a long brace with colored chalk. In front of the brace print the word "Sabbath." Back of the brace and in the top half write the word "Broken," and in the lower half the word "Kept." In front of each of these words draw another brace.

Lead the pupils to name ways in which the Sabbath is broken. Write these in the top brace; also ask how God wants His Sabbaths kept, and write the answers in the lower brace.

Let each of these be thoroughly discussed, and the lesson will develop much interest.

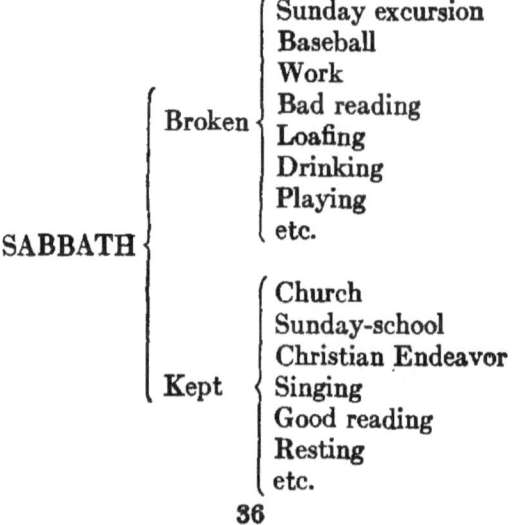

THOU SHALT NOTS
(Exod. 20: 13–17)

The following braces will prove suggestive:

Thou shalt not { Kill / Commit adultery / Steal / Bear false witness / Covet } + Christ = { A new commandment I give unto you, that ye love one another even as I have loved you.

Discuss each of the preceding commandments and have the pupils repeat them. Use the braces as a chalk-talk. Write the words "Thou shalt not"; draw a long brace in front of them; and, as the pupils repeat the commandments, write in the brace the words indicated. Draw another brace pointing to the right: in front of this write "plus Christ." Impress the lesson that after keeping all of God's commandments we must add Christ to our lives; and, if we do that, we equal the new commandment that Christ gave us. Here write John 13: 34 in an added brace.

Lead the pupils to discuss what kind of world this would be if every one kept this commandment. Let the thought of the prayer service be that God will help us to keep this greatest of all commandments.

MAN'S FAITH AND GOD'S PROMISE
(Gen. 7:1; 9:13; Heb. 11:7)

Arrange with one of the older boys to come prepared to tell the story of the flood and Noah's part in it. After this has been told have the Scripture references read.

Draw a rainbow on the blackboard. This can best be done by using the side of the chalk. If you have the colored crayons, the rainbow will be more pleasing to the children.

Write these words on the blackboard: "Noah's Faith, God's Promise." Lead the pupils to talk about each of these, also to see that having faith is trusting some one. The pupils will tell you of some one they know that they trust and tell why they trust him, or some one they do not trust. For instance, John may tell you that he knows a boy that lies and steals, and never keeps his word. On the other hand, Mary will tell you that she has a little friend that always keeps her promise, and she knows that what she says is true, and has faith in her.

Just so we have faith in God because He does just as He has promised.

The bow was God's promise to Noah that He would take care of him, and it is His promise to every one of us.

Ask the pupils to name as many of God's promises as they can remember. Write these under the bow of promise.

GIANTS AND GRASSHOPPERS
(Num. 13: 30-33)

We will make a chalk-talk of this lesson. It would be a very good plan to have two or three of your pupils meet with you and study the lesson over so that they may be able to help with the chalk-talk and read selected passages.

The story may be told somewhat as follows:

Moses sent a number of men to spy out the land of Canaan. Lead the boys and girls to tell how this was the land the Lord had promised the Israelites and to which they were travelling.

When these men came back, all but two of them were scared almost to death. They said the people in Canaan had great walled cities, and there were giants there (draw a wall with giants looking over), that the Israelites were as mere grasshoppers beside them. (Draw some grasshoppers hopping away from the wall.) These men gave a very false report about this country because they were cowards. But Caleb, one who was not afraid, said: "Come on; we can kill them, for God is with us. The land is just splendid, and flows with milk and honey." But the men who felt like grasshoppers said they were afraid to go. And the rest of the people became afraid, and were going to kill Moses and Aaron; and the Lord sent the people back into the wilderness to stay forty years.

Have one of the pupils read Num. 14: 23, 24, 36, 37. Draw a giant lying down and a grasshopper with a sword sitting on him. This is to represent how finally Caleb conquered the "giants" and was permitted to live in the land of plenty.

This lesson should teach that we should not belittle ourselves or be cowards, but that, trusting in God, we can conquer the greatest giants that we meet in our lives.

Courage, with God's aid, will conquer.

A CORD OF BLUE

(Num. 15: 37, 38, 39, first clause)

Prepare gifts to accompany this lesson as follows:

Cut some hearts from white cardboard. These should be about two inches long. Outline a cross on each, and tie a blue cord in them near the centre of the top. Have one of these for each pupil. They would look very pretty if arranged on a large card in the shape of a heart.

The following picture story may be used to illustrate the lesson. Once upon a time there was a great bridge built across a wide river. (Draw a bridge with blue chalk, and the girders of a bridge.) Strong iron supports were used, which crossed and recrossed one another. (Continue to draw the bridge.) They wanted the bridge very strong because the heavy trains would cross it loaded with human beings; and, if it should prove to be weak, there would be a terrible accident. Now, there was one piece of iron that had just a tiny crack in it; but the men who were building said, "O, that won't matter." (Draw a mark on the girders to represent the crack.)

Now that crack had a peculiar name; its name was "I forgot." So the men used the cracked iron, and it weakened the whole structure; and one sad day the bridge went down, and took with it a hundred people.

Now this bridge is our character, and the little "I forgot" is the weak spot; and sometimes it ruins not only our own lives, but other lives as well. So we need reminders. Call one of the smaller pupils to you, and tie a cord on his finger. Every child is familiar with this kind of reminder.

God gave these people a cord of blue as a reminder. He has given us a better reminder. Here lead the children to speak of the Holy Spirit as the one great reminder God gave to us. The very best reminder we can have is Christ in the heart. Here pass the hearts, and ask the children to hang them in a conspicuous place at home as a reminder of Jesus and all the things He would like to have us do.

SERPENTS

(Num. 21: 4-9; John 3: 14, 15)

Arrange the sand-board to represent the wilderness. This is done by filling it with small branches. Have this done before the meeting. Cut tents from white paper. Have one of the pupils tell how the Israelites came to be in the wilderness; another, how they were complaining because they did not have good things to eat; another, how God gave them the manna. As the lesson proceeds, complete the sand-board by arranging the tents among the trees, and sprinkle cornmeal over the ground to represent the manna. Make a "brazen serpent" by winding a piece of red or yellow yarn on a stick; or a narrow strip of tin may be cut to represent the brazen serpent; wind this on a stick.

Let the Scripture lesson be read one verse at a time; as each verse is read, draw out its central thought.

The fourth verse shows weak faith. God had been very good to them. He had fulfilled every promise, and shown them over and over that He loved them; yet they were complaining to Moses how badly God had treated them.

The fifth verse tells of their complaining. They were not satisfied with the bread or water. They said God and Moses had brought them out into the wilderness to die. Their complaining grew so loud and fierce that God took very severe means to stop it. The sixth verse tells of the fiery serpents that God sent among the people; they were very poisonous, and many people died of the serpents' bites.

The seventh verse tells that the people repented, and said, "We have sinned"; and they begged Moses to pray to God to take away the serpents. Then Moses prayed, and God heard his prayer. The eighth verse tells us that God answered the prayer. (Here set up the serpent among the tents.) Those who had been bitten by the serpents had only to look upon this brazen serpent, and the poison would leave them, and they would live. No doubt many of these people said, "O, I don't believe that thing can make me well," and turned away to die, just as many people turn from the cross of Christ and die, soul and body. Christ said, "As Moses lifted up the serpent in the wilderness, even so must the Son of man be lifted up; that whosoever believeth in him should not perish, but have eternal life" (John 3: 14, 15).

Just as the brazen serpent lifted up in the wilderness meant complete salvation to the stricken

Israelites, so Christ lifted up on the cross means complete salvation to us.

ISRAELITES	Sinned	In many ways / Before God
	Looked	At the serpent / to be cured
	Believed	In God / His promise
	Were saved	Because they looked and believed
WE	Sin	Every day / Before God
	Look	To Jesus / for eternal life
	Believe	That Jesus / can help and save
	Are saved	Because we look to Jesus

AN ANIMAL THAT TALKED
(Num. 22: 28-33)

The lesson that may be drawn from the Scripture reference is that Balaam struck and abused his beast when the poor creature was not at all to blame, and it took a miracle to show him the wrong he was doing. Just in the same way people to-day are beating and abusing their animals for what is really their own fault, and because they do not study so that they can know the real trouble.

At the previous meeting ask the pupils to be prepared to tell the different things that our animal helpers do for us, also the ways in which we can pay or cheat them. When these are drawn out in the meeting, arrange them in braces somewhat in the following manner:

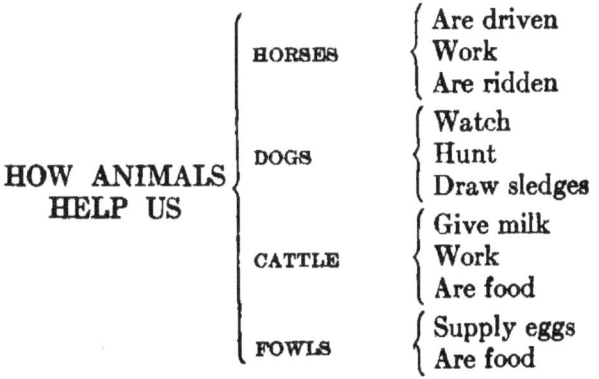

HOW WE PAY THEM	{ Treat them kindly Feed them Water them Love them etc. }
HOW WE CHEAT THEM	{ Beat them Tease them Neglect them Handle them roughly Overwork them etc. }

A MAN OF COURAGE

(Josh. 1: 1-9)

Open the lesson talk by asking the question, "What is courage?" As the pupils give the answers, write them on the blackboard. The answers will be something as follows:

It is that which helps us over hard places.

It helps us to do hard things.

It helps us to do brave things.

Print the word "Courage" on the blackboard, and draw a large brace in front of it, and by a few questions lead the pupils to fill it out as follows:

$$\text{COURAGE} \begin{cases} \text{What for?} & \begin{cases} \text{Our work} \\ \text{To live right} \\ \text{To help others} \end{cases} \\ \text{How secure it?} & \begin{cases} \text{Trust God} \\ \text{Pray for it} \\ \text{Read the Bible} \end{cases} \\ \text{Who needs it?} & \begin{cases} \text{All} \end{cases} \end{cases}$$

Outline on the blackboard a flag with a cross on it. This will work out very prettily if the flag is made white and the cross red. Under this write the words "By this we conquer."

Lead the pupils to recall persons or incidents

illustrating Christian courage, such as Daniel, the little Hebrew maid, and some of Paul's experiences. Make clear the thought that we not only need this courage for the great things in life, but we need it for the little, every-day things. These sometimes prove to be the hardest to bear, and require the most courage.

> "*Be strong to hope, O heart.*
> *Though day is bright,*
> *The stars can only shine*
> *In the dark night.*
> *Be strong, O heart of mine;*
> *Look toward the light.*
>
> "*Be strong to bear, O heart.*
> *Nothing is vain;*
> *Strive not, for life is care,*
> *And God sends pain;*
> *Heaven is above, and there*
> *Rest will remain.*
>
> "*Be strong to love, O heart.*
> *Love knows not wrong;*
> *Didst thou love, creatures even,*
> *Life were not long;*
> *Didst thou love God in heaven,*
> *Thou wouldst be strong.*"
>
> — ADELAIDE A. PROCTER

A CORD OF RED
(JOSH. 2: 12-14)

With a few questions draw from the pupils the fact that the forty years' wandering of the Israelites is nearly over; that they are now ready to cross the river Jordan. As this talk is going on, sketch some trees with green chalk, and some tents among them. Write the figures 40 over these to indicate the forty years in the wilderness. Outline the river Jordan with blue chalk at the right of the trees. Conduct the chalk-talk somewhat as follows:

After the children of Israel had wandered in the wilderness all these years they came at last to the river Jordan, in sight of the promised land. (Here draw the river.) They pitched their tents near the river, for they were afraid to cross till they had found out something about the people who lived there. (Here draw some tents along the river.) Across this river were walled cities (draw some walls) and bad people who were waiting to kill them. So Joshua said, "We will send some spies over there and find out just what these people are."

The two men set out on their perilous trip. (Draw

two men on the wall of the city, also a small house.) There was a woman that lived on the wall of the city, and these men asked her whether she would keep them overnight. Now this woman had a kind heart, and she knew the people of the land were trying to find the men so as to kill them; so she hid them in her house. The roof of her little house was covered with flax, and she took them up there, and covered them with the flax. (Make some marks on the roof of the house to represent the flax.)

The wicked men searched for them, but could not find them; so they passed on, supposing the spies had escaped. When their pursuers had gone, the woman let the spies down outside the wall with a red cord. The woman asked just one thing in return for her kindness, and that was that they would save her and all her people when they took possession of the land. The spies promised her they would, and told her to fasten in the window the red cord by which she had let them down; and, when they saw that, they would remember how kind she had been to them, and would save her and all her people. (Draw a line down from one of the windows with red chalk.)

Lead the pupils to discuss ways in which we can show kindness, what true charity means, and ways of being kind to strangers.

Teach Heb. 13:2 as a memory verse.

COURAGE, AND A BIG NOISE
(JOSH. 6: 12-20)

Arrange one end of the sand-board with some trees, hills, etc. Make a wall of large pebbles. This should be a square enclosure. Outside of this arrange the tents. Make the other end pretty with flowers, grass, and stalks of wheat or other grain. This is to represent the land of Canaan.

The Israelites had wandered for forty years in the wilderness, and now they were in sight of the promised land; but they had to overthrow the wall of Jericho before they could enter. They did not see how this could be done. The wall of Jericho was great and strong, and no ordinary measures would destroy it. So God told Joshua that they should march around that great wall and blow the trumpets, but make no other noise. Now these people had had many hard lessons, and so they did not stop and ask: "Why is not once enough? We are tired, and want to get into the land of Canaan." They were determined to win. They did not see how it was going to be done; but God said, "March around Jericho seven days," and they obeyed. When the seventh day came, they were anxious. They rose at dawn, for this day they had to go around Jericho seven times. Can we not see them? First the priests bearing the ark of the covenant; then men, women, and children, marching all day. It was no easy thing God had asked them to do, but they must obey before they could reach the promised land.

When the seventh time came, Joshua said, "Shout"; and, as the people shouted, the walls of Jericho fell, and the inhabitants inside were destroyed.

(Throw over the walls, and move the tents over into Canaan.)

The application of the lesson will bring out these facts:

We all come to a wall of Jericho in our lives. Do we meet it bravely, or do we shrink, or depend on our own strength and fail?

Sometimes God asks us to do hard things over and over just as He did with the Israelites. How should we feel when we must meet these hard things?

Sometimes God asks us to shout. He wants us to manifest our faith and proclaim our victories.

We have a promised land, and there is always a wall of Jericho to overthrow before we can pass over. He has promised to be with us and give us the victory if we will but do our part.

Ask the pupils to tell what some of our "walls of Jericho" are, and some of the victories God has helped to win.

GIDEON AND HIS BRAVE MEN
(JUDG. 6: 11–16; 8: 22, 23)

Be prepared to tell the story of Gideon and his conquest of the Midianites as told in the sixth and seventh chapters of Judges. Make the story as simple and pleasing as possible. It may be a good plan to work it into a chalk-talk. Divide the blackboard by drawing a vertical line through the centre. In one half make a great many small marks to represent the army of the Midianites. Then, as the story tells how God selected only three hundred out of the thousands of Israelites, draw three groups of men, and over each group place the figures 100. Lead the pupils to tell what these people were armed with, and how God used this army to drive away the Midianites. Over the men who represent the Israelites draw a large sword, and on it print the words "The sword of the Lord." Over the Midianites write the words "No faith in God."

The lesson to be drawn from the story will be apparent to every pupil. It is not numbers that count with God, for He could use the weak just as well if they only put their trust in Him. He can do more work with one willing little boy or girl than He can do with a whole host of unwilling people. Our lesson teaches us that God did not want any cowards. He did not want any one who was going to be afraid and run away when he saw a great number of the enemy. He just picked out the truest and bravest men among all those thousands of warriors; and just as it was then, so it is now. He may have some great work for each of us to do, and the best way to be ready for this is to keep trusting God and doing the things He tells us to do.

Teach the last part of Zech. 4:6 as a memory verse.

SAMSON

(JUDG. 13: 24; 16: 16-20)

Prepare the material for the object-lesson as follows:

Take three or four sticks, and cut a notch on them near the centre; also some string, and cut part of the strands, or, if convenient, use a small rope or twine, and cut all the strands but one in two or three places.

Ask two or three of the boys to meet with you during the week and study the story of Samson. Let each boy take an incident in his life, and be prepared to tell it at the meeting. For instance, let one tell of his physical strength; another, of the weak spot in his character; another, of how God gave him back his strength, and led him to do good work.

After the story has been duly drawn out lead the lesson talk along the lines of courage. Hold up one of the sticks, and ask how strong it is. If the pupils observe the notch in the stick, they will tell you it is not very strong because it has a notch cut in it. Break the stick, and show how that one spot weakened it, and that it was just as strong as its weakest spot. Illustrate the thought by breaking the other sticks, and in the same way by using the string or rope which has had part of the strands cut. It is just the same with people. Their characters are just as strong as their greatest weakness. We may be good and true to almost every right principle, and yet have one little sin in our lives which spoils it all; for we are no stronger anywhere in our lives than we are at that little sinful place in our characters.

Ask the pupils whether they ever knew any one who tried to cover up wrong things in his life by doing good things in the sight of man. Bring out the thought of how so many men get their great wealth by pinching and overworking poor men, women, and children. Some of these men give great gifts to charity and other good causes, but that does not make them right in the sight of God. They are no stronger, because they have a notch of sin in their characters.

Ask how we can strengthen the notches in our character. Ask one of the pupils to read Judg. 16: 28, and teach that, just as Samson called on the Lord for strength, and had his prayer answered, so we can call on the Lord to strengthen the weak spots in our character with just as sure results.

RUTH, A LOVING DAUGHTER
(RUTH 1: 14–18; 2: 11, 12)

By following either of the following suggestions one can make a very appropriate gift to the pupils to accompany this lesson. Get pictures of "The Gleaners" or "Ruth," or prepare a gift for each pupil as follows: Take small cards, or cut light cardboard or heavy paper into cards. Cut two parallel slits about a quarter of an inch apart, and through them slip a head of oats, wheat, or some other grain. On the card place the following brace:

RUTH $\begin{cases} \text{Self-sacrificing} \\ \text{Industrious} \\ \text{Faithful} \end{cases}$

By taking a brief forecast of the lesson the preceding Sunday the pupils will be prepared to make the story of Ruth very interesting, as it is one of the favorite Bible stories. Let the following characteristics be made impressive.

Ruth left her home and her people to go to a distant land in order to take care of her mother-in-law. She had no selfish interest. There was no pleasure in leaving all that she held dear to go among strangers and work for a living.

When they reached Bethlehem, where Naomi's people lived, Ruth set right to work to earn a living for her mother-in-law. She worked from morning till night in the hot sun, and because she was so industrious she won friends who helped her throughout her life.

She was very kind and thoughtful for others.

Write the words "How can we be like Ruth?" on the blackboard, and after them draw a brace. Let the pupils name helpful things we can do which the lesson of Ruth suggests to them.

A BOY WHO WORKED FOR GOD
(1 Sam. 2: 18, 26)

Have a small Christmas candle to represent Samuel. Make clear to the pupils that Samuel was only a little boy at this time. He had been cared for by a God-fearing mother. He was getting ready to do a great service for God. Samuel knew nothing about this; yet, when God called, he answered and said, "Speak, for thy servant heareth."

Light the little candle, and tell the pupils that it represents Samuel, for he was the only light in a dark place. This little boy was the only spark of good among a sinful people.

Illustrate this by the missionaries. They leave all, and go to a heathen country. Sometimes they cannot even speak the language of the people with whom they live. They are the only spark of God in a dark country, among people uneducated and often cruel. Speak of Rev. John G. Paton, who went many years ago as a missionary to the New Hebrides. He was a tiny spot of light, but the light grew and grew till now there are many lights there.

Leave the pupils to review the story of Samuel and Eli.

Ask the questions "What can we do for God?" "What can we do in His house?" As the pupils give the answers, let these be discussed thoroughly. They will bring out the lessons of worship, reverence, faithfulness, prayerfulness, and sacredness.

A LITTLE MESSENGER
(1 Sam. 3: 11–18)

Prepare the sand-board by spreading the sand level over the board. In the centre place a small candle, and on each corner a sign-board, which may consist of a toothpick with a small square of paper slipped over the end. On these print the abbreviations for north, south, east, and west. Have four extra candles. As the lesson story is told, light the candle in the centre of the board, which will represent Samuel, as in the preceding lesson.

The Lord made a messenger out of Samuel. He had a special work for him to do and a special mission in the world for him. He has the same for each one of us.

Make clear the thought of Samuel's willingness to be a messenger for God. Call attention to the little light on the sand-board. It is shining as far as it can; but over here, north, south, east, and west, are people who are in darkness that this little light cannot reach. How can we be messengers for God, and take a light to them? Make a path from the candle in the centre to each of the sign-cards. Then light the four candles from the centre light, and place one on each corner of the board. We may not be able to take the light ourselves; and, if not, how can we help to send the light? Let the pupils discuss this part of the lesson.

Close the lesson talk by summing up the lessons we have learned from Samuel.

Let the thought of the prayer service be that we may prepare ourselves to be God's messengers as faithfully as Samuel prepared. Pictures of little Samuel would be an appropriate gift to accompany this lesson.

Have the pupils sum up the lesson in an acrostic. The following is suggested:

      S erved
      A nswered
      M inded
      U seful
      E steemed
      L oved

A KING GOD CHOSE

(1 Sam. 10: 20–25)

At the previous meeting ask the pupils to learn all they can about Saul during the week.

After the reading of the Scripture lesson ask the pupils to name all the Bible kings they can think of. Write these on the blackboard, and after Saul's name make a brace. Draw from the pupils what they have learned about Saul, and condense their suggestions into a word or sentence, and place this in the brace.

Lead the pupils to discuss each characteristic as it is named. A few well-chosen questions will add to the interest.

Ask the pupils what other king God chose. Lead them to name Jesus. Print this word on the blackboard, and after it make a brace. Lead the pupils to tell why God chose Christ for a king. As the reasons are suggested, write them in the brace. Make clear that God has chosen us to do His work just as He chose Saul; that each of us may be a king or queen in God's sight if we will but carry on His work; that our crowns are awaiting us, and all we have to do is to make ourselves worthy of them. Some will lose their crowns as Saul did. Let the thought of the prayer service be that we may be worthy to be crowned.

Teach Matt. 25:23 for a memory verse.

A PRINCE WHO WAS TRUE
(1 Sam. 14: 6-42)

The materials for the gifts will consist of some white or tinted cardboard and some pretty cord. Cut from the cardboard some hearts, anchors, and crosses. These should be about three inches long and wide in proportion. Tie an anchor, a heart, and a cross together by looping a piece of cord about them. On the heart write the word "Myself"; on the anchor, "My Faith"; and on the cross, "My Saviour." Prepare one of these for each pupil. They would make a very pleasing appearance if fastened to a piece of dark cardboard or pasteboard covered with black cloth.

Draw from the pupils the story of the lesson, how Saul, in cowardly fear, would not meet the enemy, and how Jonathan the prince and friend of David, went forward with only his armor-bearer, and put the enemy to flight. Make clear the lesson of Jonathan's faith in God, also of how God will always help His children when they are trying to overcome their enemies, sin and wrong.

Have the gifts passed among the pupils, and

OLD TESTAMENT STORIES 69

use them as an object-lesson, teaching that the hearts represent ourselves; we can make them good or bad; but, if we let in faith, which is represented by the anchor, that leads us to the cross of Christ; then, with these three, ourselves, our faith, and our Saviour, we can overcome every enemy that we may meet.

The following Bible readings are suggested to follow the lesson:

Isa. 35: 9.	Jer. 31: 28.
Isa. 40: 11.	Zeph. 3: 17.
Isa. 40: 29.	Zech. 4: 6.
Isa. 40: 31.	Isa. 45: 2.
Isa. 42: 13.	Isa. 49: 9.
Isa. 42: 16.	Isa. 54: 17.
Isa. 43: 2.	Jer. 30: 11.
Matt. 10: 29.	1 Cor. 10: 13.
Matt. 24: 31.	2 Thess. 3: 3.
Luke 21: 18.	Rev. 3: 10.
Rom. 8: 28.	1 Pet. 3: 12.

GOD'S TEST
(1 Sam. 16: 6-12)

Use for the object-lesson an apple that appears perfect and sound on the outside, but has a bad, worm-eaten heart. The apple can be cut in two to find out its condition, and be fastened together again with toothpicks. Also have a perfect apple, but not quite so large or nice-looking as the other.

These were all good-looking men that passed in front of God, but He did not choose any of them. Now, there was some reason.

Here make clear to the pupils that God can see us through and through; that He knows every thought of our minds and every motive, whether good or bad. He could see right down into these men's hearts, and he saw that they were bad.

Now show the apple with the bad heart; hold it up and ask whether it looks good to eat, and which of the two is the better-looking. Compare it to the men who passed before God. Now open the apple, and show the bad heart.

Let one of the pupils tell the story of how the heart of the apple became bad; how, when it was a beautiful blossom on the apple-tree, a tiny fly came buzzing along and left a little egg right in the heart of the blossom. Soon the petals fell off; and, where the blossom had been, there grew a little apple; but, as the apple grew, the egg hatched into a little worm that finally ate the heart away, and then bored its way out. Compare this story of the apple with our own lives. The little germ of sin enters into our hearts sometimes merely as a pleasure, but it grows and grows until our hearts are all bad.

But there was one man who passed before God who had a good heart. Here show the perfect apple; open it; and show the good heart.

Close the lesson with the following questions:
How shall we look as we pass before God?
Will He choose us?

A BOY AND A GIANT
(1 Sam. 17: 4-11, 32-37)

Arrange with one of the boys a week before to tell the story of David and Goliath. Make a chalk-talk of this; and, as the story is being told, draw on the blackboard figures to represent David with his sling and Goliath with his armor and sword. It would be well to have the boy who tells the story illustrate it with a sling-shot and five small stones.

Liken the giant Goliath to the giant Sin, and David to one of the pupils.

Now, each one of us is like David, and has started out to kill the giant. David tried on Saul's armor, but it was so large and clumsy that he said he never could kill the giant with that on; so he took it off, and took out of his shepherd's bag a sling. Now, David thought a good deal of that sling; for he had killed wild animals with it, and felt sure that he could kill Goliath; so he hunted around and found five smooth little stones, then went to meet the giant. Now, the giant was covered with armor; there was just one place where the stone from David's sling could strike, and that was just under the giant's helmet.

The giant made fun of David, and called him a dog; but he did not laugh long, for David whirled his sling around, and the little stone sped away to strike the giant down.

Now what can we have that David had when we go to kill our giant?

First, we can have faith in God; second, we can have courage; third, we can have love for right; fourth, we can want to rid the land of the bad giant.

What can we have that David did not have? (Draw a cross on the blackboard, and make it plain to the pupils that we have Christ, our friend and elder brother, who is always ready to help us overthrow the giant Sin.)

A ROYAL FRIENDSHIP
(1 Sam. 20: 11-17)

Once upon a time a tall and beautiful knight made a vow to search for the Holy Grail till he found it. So he put on his gilded mail that sparkled so brightly it looked like a blazing sheaf. He was young and strong, and had never known any sadness or gloom in his life; and with a light heart he sprang upon his dark charger, and started on his quest.

As he passed through the dark gate that led out from the castle, he saw a leper crouched down by the stones, moaning and begging with his hands outstretched. The knight shrunk away from him in loathing, for he was repelled and angered at the sight of the ragged beggar; so he scornfully tossed the leper a piece of gold, and went dashing away on his charger.

The leper did not touch the gold, but said,

"*'Better to me the poor man's crust,*
Better the blessing of the poor,
Though I turn me empty from his door;
That is no true alms which the hand can hold;

*He gives only the worthless gold
Who gives from a sense of duty;
But he who gives but a slender mite,
And gives to that which is out of sight, —
That thread of the all-sustaining Beauty
Which runs through all and doth all unite, —
The hand cannot clasp the whole of his alms,
The heart outstretches its eager palms,
For a god goes with it, and makes it store
To the soul that was starving in darkness before.'"*

The trees were bare, and the boughs rattled shudderingly. Winter had shrouded the earth.

"*An old, bent man, worn out and frail,
He came back from seeking the Holy Grail.*"

He was thinly clad, with a look of pain and suffering in his face, and his steps tottered. He sat down at the gate of the castle that was no longer his, but belonged to another; and, as he sat there thinking over the days gone by, the loathsome leper again stood beside him, saying,

"*For Christ's sweet sake I beg an alms*";

and the knight, looking at him, said,

"' *I behold in thee
An image of Him who died on the tree;
Thou also hast had thy crown of thorns;
Thou also hast had the world's buffets and scorns;*

*And to thy life were not denied
The wounds in the hands and feet and side;
Mild Mary's Son, acknowledge me;
Behold, through him I give to Thee!'"*

And the knight broke in two his single crust, and gave half to the leper; then he went to the stream, and brought a drink of water.

*"And the voice that was softer than silence said
'Lo, it is I; be not afraid.
In many climes, without avail,
Thou hast spent thy life for the Holy Grail;
Behold, it is here — this cup which thou
Didst fill at the streamlet for me but now;
This crust is My body broken for thee,
This water His blood that died on the tree.*

. . . .

*Who gives himself with his alms feeds three, —
Himself, his hungering neighbor, and Me.'"*
— JAMES RUSSELL LOWELL
From "The Vision of Sir Launfal."

A GIFT THAT GOD LIKES
(2 SAM. 24: 18-25)

Make five cards about nine inches square; these should be made of heavy paper or light-weight cardboard. On the first card draw a safe, or paste on it the picture of a safe; and over it print the words "God's Safe." On the second card draw some picture to represent money; on the third, the figure of a girl with a broom in her hand; on the fourth, some boys playing ball; and on the fifth, a heart. Make a hole in the centre of the top of each of the cards, and tie them together loosely with a narrow ribbon or cord.

After the reading of the Scripture lesson begin the lesson talk by telling how we all have things that we value very highly, and we want to put them in a safe place.

Here show the first card, and by a few questions lead the pupils to tell about different kinds of safes and their uses. Then call attention to the words over the picture, and ask what things we have that we should like to keep safe. The pupils will be almost sure to name money; then show the second card, and ask how we can put our money into God's safe. This will lead to a discussion of benevolent giving, and the pupils will draw the lesson that giving our money to the church, the Sunday-school, Christian Endeavor, and missionary work is putting it in God's safe.

The third card will teach us a lesson of making our every-day work a service to God; by doing it cheerfully and well we are putting a rich treasure into God's safe.

The fourth card will bring out the lesson that we can make our play and amusements of service, because they will help to make us strong for the work we have to do.

But the thing God wants most is our hearts. Here show a picture of the heart, and bring out the thought of consecrating ourselves to God and placing our hearts in His safe keeping.

Let the thought of the prayer service be that God will help us to give ourselves unreservedly to Him.

> *"A servant with this clause*
> *Makes drudgery divine;*
> *Who sweeps a room as for Thy laws*
> *Makes that and the action fine."*
> — GEORGE HERBERT

THE LORD'S HOUSE
(I KINGS 8: 22-30)

Once upon a time there were two boys who were about to go to a king's house. Now, the king lived in a magnificent palace that had about it beautiful trees and flowers; and inside the floors were white and clean and the windows of the most delicate glass.

The boys were very glad to go to the king's house, nor did they feel afraid, because they had heard that the king was a very good man, and loved little children very dearly.

When they arrived at the king's house, one of the boys cleaned his shoes very neatly, dusted his cap, and entered very quietly. The other boy was in such a hurry to see what was inside that he went dashing up the marble steps without giving a thought to his soiled shoes or how he might look. The first boy after entering the king's house sat down very quietly and listened to the king's servant, who was giving a message from the king; but the second boy did not seem to care anything about the message, and was noisy and rude. He scuffled his feet about, making much noise and soiling the floor; then he rolled up some paper wads, and threw them at the other boy; and, not quite satisfied with this, he even ventured to throw one at the king's servant.

Soon he grew tired of this, and began to search in his pockets to see whether he had anything else to play with. He found some beans, and began throwing them at the windows, and broke some of the beautiful glass; then he found some peanuts, and ate them, throwing the shells on the floor, and kept whispering and laughing and spoiling the beautiful home of the king; and, besides being rude and ungentlemanly, he failed to hear the beautiful message from the king, while the other boy had been good and listened to all the king's servant had said; and, when he went home, he told his mother that the king had said in his message that he loved them and was going to bring them all to live in a beautiful mansion where they would never have to sorrow or toil as they were doing.

The second boy did not have any happy message to take home, for he had not heard it.

After the story has been read lead the pupils to see that these two boys were like many children going to church. The church is the king's home, and the first boy was like those who come for a good purpose and to listen to God's message; the second, like those who are careless and do everything to spoil God's house and disturb the meetings. Teach the following verse as a memory gem:

*"What kind of a church would my church be
If every member was just like me?"*

GOD'S BIRDS
(1 KING 17: 5, 6; LUKE 12: 24)

Two weeks previous to this meeting ask the pupils each to write a story about birds. This alone will give you ample material for a full meeting. In case you may not have enough to fill out the class hour the following suggestions will help.

How can we protect our song-birds?

This will lead to a discussion about sparing the lives of the birds, not shooting or otherwise injuring them for mere pastime, not robbing or destroying their nests or killing their young, etc.

How should we care for our winter birds and those that come to us in the early spring?

From this develop the thought of feeding the birds when the snow is on the ground and all their natural food covered up. Several plans are suggested; for instance, one lady grinds all her stale bread-crusts, and keeps the crumbs in a can, and throws out a handful to the birds every winter morning. The early robins and large birds are very fond of your apple-cores and parings, and a choice morsel for the sparrows and snowbirds is a soup-bone or a piece of suet laid in the crotch of a tree.

How should we care for our pet birds?

Be thoughtful to water them, and always keep cuttlebone or a little sand in the cage. Do not feed them cakes or sweets, but occasionally a morsel of apple or lettuce-leaf.

We should never wear birds on our hats. This fashion has led to the destruction of thousands upon thousands of the beautiful birds of the tropics, until many species are quite extinct. In many cases the only time when these birds can be captured is at the nesting-season, when the mother bird is ruthlessly taken and the young left to starve and die.

AN UNHAPPY KING
(1 Kings 21: 1-4)

Previously arrange with your pupils for each to bring some choice fruit to this meeting. One may bring a bunch of grapes; another, two or three peaches; another, a pear, etc. Provide a basket for the fruit; a very pretty one can be made from a peach-basket covered and lined with colored tissue-paper. As the fruit is brought, place it in the basket, and use it for an object-lesson.

The pupils should be told that the fruit is to be sent to those in a hospital or to other sick persons. Now have the story of the lesson read or told, about how Ahab coveted the vineyard and became so unhappy about it that it made him sick and disagreeable. Draw from the pupils the lesson that we should be just like Ahab if we coveted the basket of fruit, and wanted to eat it ourselves instead of taking it to the sick. This thought can be enlarged and the lesson on covetousness made very clear. Other illustrations may be used; for instance, if we see another person have something new or pretty, and want it ourselves, we are covetous.

Ask the pupils whether they have wanted anything that they saw some one else have, or whether they have begged mother or father to get them something like what some one else had, and then became unhappy because their parents did not feel that it would be best to get it.

Make clear the thought that perhaps more people are made unhappy because they want, and try to get, things like what other people have than in any other way.

Write the Ten Commandments on the blackboard, and teach them for a memory selection.

PERSEVERANCE
(2 KINGS 13: 14–19)

Arrange with the boys of your society to meet with you and make some bows and arrows, one for each pupil. The bow should be made of a flexible twig or stick about seven or eight inches long, and a common cord can be used for a bowstring. The arrows may be made of strawberry-boxes, and the word "Victory" may be printed on the large end. The arrow should be tacked or fastened to the bow with a pin which can be pushed through and bent up out of the way.

Have the lesson story clearly brought out and discussed. Print the word "Perseverance" on the blackboard, and after it a brace; then ask the pupils to tell what perseverance means; for instance,

PERSEVERANCE
{
Never give up
Keep right on fighting
Determination
Pluck
Unconquerable
}

Ask the pupils to name instances of perseverance. Recall the Revolutionary War, the Panama Canal, and Martin Luther.

How Can We Gain the Victory over { Sin, Our enemies, Ourselves, Our sorrows?

Tell the pupils to hang up the bow with the arrow where it will be a reminder of perseverance and victory every time they look at it.

THE BRAVE QUEEN
(Esth. 4: 16)

At the previous meeting ask the pupils to read carefully the book of Esther, and select some one to tell the story of Esther found in the first three chapters; another, that of Haman; and another, that of Mordecai.

Draw a crown on the blackboard to represent Queen Esther's crown, and on the points of the crown make some "gems" by using chalk of different colors. The projection in the centre should be longer than those on the sides. Lead the pupils to tell you what it was that led Queen Esther to appear before the king. They will mention courage. Write this word above the large gem in the crown, and discuss this trait of character with the pupils. Ask them to mention other things that go to make a strong character such as Queen Esther displays in the lesson. Such words as "Loyalty," "Truth," etc., may be written above the other gems in the crown.

Write the words "Dare to do right" on the blackboard, and lead the pupils to tell of other people who have dared to do right. Make it clear that Queen Esther had no selfish purpose in doing what she did. On the other hand, she knew that it might mean death to her, that if she displeased the king he would surely punish her; but for the sake of the people she loved she dared to do what was right; and God kept her from being punished.

MORDECAI, THE FAITHFUL
(Esth. 6: 1-11)

For the object-lesson use a white heart with the word "Faithful" printed across it.

Have one of the girls tell the story of Mordecai, and after that lead the pupils to compare his character with that of Haman.

As the pupils name fruits of faithfulness, have them written on lines radiating from the heart.

Rudely sketch a scaffold and a cross. Bring out clearly the end of each of these men, and how one thought only of self and the other thought only of doing right. Write the word "Punishment" across the scaffold and the word "Reward" on the cross.

Bring in the thought that it is faithfulness that makes true Christian Endeavor, that because of this quality Christian Endeavor has lived so many years to bless thousands of young people. Also make it clear to the pupils that it rests with the children of to-day whether Christian Endeavor will be a living power twenty-five years hence.

Faithful pupils make faithful Endeavorers.

THE BIBLE-LOVER'S PSALM
(Ps. 1)

Begin the lesson by having a short talk with the pupils about the Psalms and their author. The word "psalm" means a song to be sung to a stringed instrument like a lyre. Sketch a lyre on the blackboard. This is one of the most ancient and most harmonious of musical instruments. David used it a great deal in singing the psalms that he had composed.

A very pretty gift to accompany this lesson could be made by sketching a lyre on a small card, and under it printing the reference, Ps. 1.

The object-lesson will consist of the picture of a large tree and some chaff. Let the tree represent those in whom the Lord delights. Lead the pupils to speak of the fruitfulness of trees. Ask what the earth would be like without any trees on it. We should have no shade, no wood, no apples or oranges; the squirrels would have no homes, and the birds no place for their nests or shelter from the storms.

Now show the chaff, and ask the pupils what it is good for. The farmer always tries to get rid of the chaff. He puts his grain through a machine that will blow the chaff away, because it is good for nothing, and spoils the grain if left in. It is so with the wicked. God separates them from the righteous because He has no use for them, and David says, "The way of the wicked shall perish."

Sum up the lesson with the question, "What must we do if we would be fruitful like the tree, and what must we avoid doing if we would not be like the chaff?" The answers as given by the pupils may be written on the blackboard.

THE TWENTY-THIRD PSALM

The following object-lesson has been much used; but it is ever pleasing to the pupils, and I think will be very appropriate to the lesson of to-day. Take a glass pitcher or clear glass vase and five glasses. The glasses should contain just enough water to make the pitcher overflow when they are emptied into it. Have clear water in four of the glasses and water that has been colored red with red dye or ink in the fifth. The pitcher should be set on a plate or in a dish. The pitcher will represent our lives, and the glasses of water the good things that God has put into them. So, as a glass of water is held up, let the pupils name some of the good things that God is continually putting into our lives. Then pour the water into the pitcher, and do so with each glass of water. Lead the thought to the greatest blessing that God ever gave to man. The pupils will tell you that it is Jesus, that with this blessing go all the other gifts that are mentioned in our Scripture lesson, and that, when Christ comes into the life, it is beautified and made strong and good, and made to overflow with happiness and love. At this point pour the red liquid into the pitcher. This represents Christ in our lives, and the overflow impresses the thought that our lives overflow with God's blessings. "My cup runneth over" with good things.

Let the pupils repeat the twenty-third Psalm in concert, and also John 3: 16.

A PSALM OF PRAISE
(Ps. 103)

Plan the lesson a week or two before. Ask the pupils to bring their Bibles, also one object for which we should be thankful. The objects should be very simple, such as flowers, apples, a piece of bread, etc.

Have the music committee arrange with reference to the praise service.

The Scripture lesson is too long to be read by the teacher, as the pupils grow restless and inattentive. It may be divided into four or five parts and given to the different committees, each committee rising and reading in concert the part of the lesson assigned to them.

Have some simple prayers written on slips of paper. Give these to those pupils who are diffident about praying aloud. Then, as the pupils name the different ways in which we can praise God, let each one be demonstrated. For instance, we praise God in our songs. Then let two or three songs be sung. We praise God by telling others about Him. Follow this with some testimonies about Jesus.

We praise God in prayer. Ask that each pupil make a short prayer. We praise God with our lives. Then follow with a brief talk about how we can praise God with our lives.

The following braces are suggestive:

PRAISE GOD
- For benefits
  - Home
  - Friends
  - etc.
- For forgiveness — Ps. 86:5
- For salvation — John 3:16
- For loving-kindness
  - Comfort
  - Blessings
  - etc.

A LESSON FROM THE LONGEST PSALM
(Ps. 119: 9-16)

Begin the lesson with a talk about laws — by whom they are made, what they are for, etc. If you have been able to secure a law-book, show it to the pupils, and lead them to talk freely of what they know about the laws of their country or town. Then lead the thought to God's laws. Have the pupils turn to the book of Leviticus, and explain to them how these were the first laws given to the children of Israel by God. Call attention to the Ten Commandments. These are also some of God's laws.

Make it clear that the reason why God made laws for people to obey was because He knew there would be many things that it would not be best for us to do. So in these laws He has told us what these things are.

David says in the lesson that he rejoices in God's laws and meditates on them, and that he will not forget God's word. This is what God expects of all of us.

How can we know most about God's laws?

How can we best learn to obey them?

What will happen to us if we do not obey them?

What will God give us if we do obey them?

TRUST

(Prov. 3: 5, 6)

After the reading of the Scripture lesson give a brief talk about what it means to trust. The pupils will tell you that they trust their parents. Ask them why they trust their parents. How do they know that there will be food for them to-morrow, and new clothes when they need them? Do we trust God in the same way?

Sometimes we say that God does not answer our prayers. Make clear to the pupils that God always answers prayers, but that He does not always answer them in the way we expect. Sometimes God says, "No," just as our parents do. If it is good for us, they will give to us what we ask; but, if they do not think it is good for us, they will say, "No"; and God treats us in the same way. If a thing is good for us, He gives it; but if not, He says, "No."

Ask the pupils to name some things that God gives us. They will name the sunshine, rain, our sleep, etc. If we can trust Him for these, why not trust Him for all things?

Make a large brace on the blackboard, and ask the pupils to name some things that show God's thought and care for us. Write these in the brace. In another brace write some reasons why we should trust God, as they are mentioned by the pupils.

Have the pupils turn to the sixth chapter of Matthew and read the story of how God cares for the birds and the flowers of the field.

The following references may be used as a Bible reading:

Ps. 40: 4.	Ps. 118: 8.
Ps. 146: 3.	Prov. 3: 5.
Ps. 91: 2.	Ps. 23: 1.
Ps. 11: 1.	Ps. 7: 1.
Prov. 29: 25.	Ps. 62: 8.
2 Chron. 20: 20.	Ps. 5: 11.

OUR WORDS
(Prov. 15: 1-4)

Illustrate the following story with chalk and blackboard as it is being told. Sketch the figures rapidly, and do not stop for detail or artistic effect.

Once upon a time there were two boys who lived on the same street (draw a horizontal line to represent a street). The boy that lived on the right-hand side of the street was named Phil, and the one on the left-hand side of the street, Harry. (Sketch the two boys on the blackboard, giving Phil a pleasing countenance by turning the corners of his mouth upward, and Harry a cross look by turning the corners of his mouth downward.)

Now, Phil and Harry were jolly good boys, and usually had pretty good times; but there was one difference between them. Phil always had a smile on his face and a pleasant answer for every one; but Harry was sour and cross, and, if he did not feel just right, his answers were apt to be harsh and unpleasant.

One day the boys went nutting, and they had just found a fine hickory-tree over the fence in

Mr. Brown's field. (Draw a tree.) Now, of course, these boys, like most boys, never thought about whom the nuts might belong to. So over the fence they went, and Phil climbed to the very top of the tree to shake down the nuts. The nuts were just rattling down over Harry's head when a man came along the road (draw a man on the road) and said to Harry, "These are pretty nice hickory-nuts, aren't they, my boy?"

"None of your business," said Harry.

The man looked astonished, but said quietly, "I suppose, of course, you asked Mr. Brown whether you could gather these nuts."

"No, I didn't," replied Harry; "and I don't intend to, either. He's an old crosspatch, and he'll never know who took his nuts."

Now, Phil had been busily shaking the nuts, and had heard only Harry's last remark. He looked down through the leaves, and saw the gentleman, and at once remembering Harry's disposition, climbed down the tree, walked up to Mr. Brown, and, raising his hat politely, said, "Do these nuts belong to you, Mr. Brown?"

Now, Mr. Brown was at once struck with the difference in the way in which the two boys had addressed him; and, as he looked into Phil's frank, honest eyes, he thought, "There is a boy who will grow up to be a good, honest man"; but he only said to Phil, "Yes, I own the tree, but I am willing to share the nuts with a boy who is as polite and genteel as you are, but I do not think I have any nuts for a boy that cannot give a civil answer."

Then, turning to Harry, the gentleman said: "My boy, you will learn one thing as you go through life, that 'a soft answer turneth away wrath, but a grievous word stirreth up anger.' If in a year from now you have learned to give a pleasant answer when you are spoken to, come with your bag, and I will share my nuts with you; but to-day I have none for you. You may go." Then, turning to Phil, he said, "Fill your bag with nuts, my boy, and remember that Mr. Brown is always willing to share his nuts with a boy who proves himself to be always honest and pleasant to others."

KNOWN BY OUR DEEDS
(Prov. 20: 11)

We will make a chalk-talk of this lesson. First draw a man, or the face of a man, giving it a sour look by turning the corners of the mouth downward. Ask the pupils whether they ever saw such a person with a bad temper, and lead them to tell some of the deeds such persons do. Also draw a man with a beer-bottle. This will symbolize a drunkard. The pupils will tell you that he is a bully, and that his deeds are not good. Make some round figures to represent marbles, and lead the pupils to see that the first lessons in dishonesty begin with playing for keeps. Draw some playing-cards. These will represent the deeds of the gambler. Draw a girl with a new dress to represent pride.

All the figures above will lead to the talk about our bad deeds. Now draw a man with a Bible; another, with a basket to represent kindness. Draw a boy with a smiling face and a man with a cross. These represent truthfulness and helpfulness.

The ships that cross the seas back and forth,

and pass one another, always know to what country they belong: for each ship carries its own flag, and, just as the ships are known by the flags they carry, so we are known by the deeds we do. Sometimes a pirate ship will carry a false flag so as to cover up its deeds; so some people try to cover up their deeds by an outward show of being good; but, just as the pirate ship is always found out, so our bad deeds are always found out.

Teach Rom. 2: 6 as a memory verse.

"REMEMBER THY CREATOR"
(Eccl. 12:1)

Things to remember	{ To do good To pray To love
If God forgot	{ To send rain To send sunshine To hear our prayers
What Reminders Have We?	{ Bible Flowers Food etc.
Why Remember God while Young?	{ He remembers us We should give Him our best
How Can We Help Others to Remember Him?	{ Tell them Love them Pray for them Help them

One way to remember God is to commit to memory a part of the book He has given us. Have the pupils repeat as many Bible verses as they can remember. It would be a good plan to arrange with them to commit to memory one or more verses every week, and repeat them at the meetings. Ask that each one commit to memory the lesson text.

THE LITTLE FOXES
(Song of Sol. 2: 15)

The following object-lesson may be given by a pupil to illustrate the lesson topic. You will need for it a glass of water and a little ink in a bottle. Let the pupil go forward, hold up the glass of water, and liken it to our lives. It is pure and clear and good, like our lives before sin comes into them. Then let the pupil put one drop of ink into the glass of water, and draw the illustration that just as the drop of ink has spoiled the water for usefulness, so a little sin will spoil our lives and unfit them for the great usefulness that God meant them.

After the object-lesson the superintendent may make a brief talk, or, better still, lead the pupils to tell about some of the "little foxes" that spoil our lives; and this may be taken up and talked about.

GOD'S PROPHETS AND THEIR MESSAGE
(JER. 25: 4-7)

Our lessons now go into the books of the prophets, and in order that you may be able to help the pupils it would be a good plan to find out all you can about the prophets yourself, who they were, when they lived, their mission, etc. A good Bible dictionary will be a great help in this. The following card, if carefully prepared and hung up in the room, will be a great help in these lessons, and will fix the names of the prophets permanently in the minds of the pupils. The card should be white and placed in a frame or on a board to keep it in shape. Then print plainly in large letters the names of the prophets.

The following list may be used:

Jonah	Nahum	Obadiah
Joel	Zephaniah	Ezekiel
Amos	Jeremiah	Haggai
Hosea	Habbakuk	Zechariah
Isaiah	Daniel	Malachi
Micah		

Make clear to the pupils what a prophecy is. Use the common illustrations, the prophecy of the weather. Speak of the United States Weather Bureau, which prophesies the weather for every day.

Lead the pupils to tell what kind of men the prophets were. By using the card the pupils will recall many of the prophets, and be able to tell something about them.

In the following lessons found in the books of the prophets make it a point to have the pupils become acquainted with each one of them. Too often our children are left ignorant of these splendid men and their messages to us.

ISAIAH TELLS ABOUT CHRIST
(ISA. 53: 1-12)

A pretty gift to accompany this lesson can be made by outlining on cards of the size of a calling-card, cut from cardboard or heavy paper, a cross, on which print the motto "Remember Jesus Christ" (2 Tim. 2: 8).

By this time the pupils will understand pretty well what a prophecy is; but it would be a good plan to talk it over again, so that they may have a clear understanding of just what this fifty-third of Isaiah means, that more than seven hundred years before Christ came to the world God put it into Isaiah's heart to tell the story of His life.

Have the chapter read very carefully, and lead the pupils to see how it all came to pass just as Isaiah told it.

As the first verse of the chapter is read, ask one of the pupils to turn to Luke 7: 22 and read the verse. This will show the pupils how these verses answer Isaiah's question.

Then have the first half of the second verse followed by Luke 2: 52, then the second half of the second verse by Mark 6:3. Compare verses 3-8, inclusive, with Mark 15:1-5 and Luke 22:63-65. Then have the ninth verse read, followed by Luke 23:33, 50-53, and verses 10-12 followed by Luke 24:50-52.

After these have been read compare the two stories, that in Isaiah with the one in the New Testament that has been read. The pupils will be very quick to see that they are exactly alike, that Isaiah foresaw the life of the Son of God as He would live it in this world.

This will also make clear to the pupils that years and years before Christ came God was planning to send us a Redeemer. This will lead to a quiet talk about the great love that God had for us in giving His only begotten Son for our Saviour.

THE SABBATH; HOW MAKE IT A DAY OF DELIGHT
(ISA. 58: 13, 14)

Have one of your committees meet with you during the week before this meeting and prepare two calendars as follows:

Get two pieces of cardboard nine by twelve inches, and on each make a calendar to represent the one-day calendars that are used in offices. The top of the calendar may be decorated with a drawing or simply a pleasing and attractive picture. Below this print the word "Sunday." Under this on one calendar write the word "*Kept*," and on the other, the word "*Broken*." Take these to the meeting, together with a black crayon or pencil that will make a broad mark. After the reading of the Scripture lesson show the calendars; tell the pupils that the calendars represent our Sabbaths, and that we are going to name ways to keep the Sabbath as God would have us keep it, and ways in which the Sabbath is broken.

Appoint two of your pupils who can print or write well; and, as the others name ways of keeping or breaking the Sabbath, have them written neatly on the calendars. After these are filled hang them side by side on the wall of the room. The suggestions on them will lead to a general talk on the subject "How can we make the Sabbath a delight?"

CALLED OF GOD: JEREMIAH, OURSELVES

(JER. 1: 6-10)

If possible, get three acorns to use as the object-lesson.

After the reading of the Scripture lesson show the acorns, and bring out the thought that they contain a germ of life, very small, to be sure, and if placed in the ground will grow into trees, strong and large and beautiful.

Draw a wide mark across the blackboard to represent soil or earth. This can be done by using the side of the chalk. In this soil draw an acorn with a tiny sprout coming from it. Liken this to Jeremiah as he started when only a little boy to do God's work. Extend the sprout into a tree with several branches, and let the pupils name some of the things that Jeremiah's life stood for. As they are named, write them on the tree.

"Plant" another acorn in the soil on the blackboard, and liken it to Christ's life. Let one of the pupils tell the story of His boyhood, how He "grew and waxed strong." As you draw the tree, let it take the shape of a cross; and on the arms of the cross write some of the deeds of Christ's life as they are suggested by the pupils. Then plant another acorn. This will stand for the pupils. From this make a tree. Let the pupils name things they can do as they wax strong and grow into men and women.

Let the following lessons be drawn:

God "plants" us for some purpose of His own, and we can grow into good, useful persons as Jeremiah did.

The call comes to us just as plainly as it came to the prophet. We often try to excuse ourselves by saying we are too young, or something of the kind; but God will not excuse us. We have the same promise that He made to Jeremiah, "Be not afraid, for I am with thee to deliver thee."

Have the pupils use verse 7 as a memory verse, and follow with a prayer-service in which the thought may be that God will help us to be ready to do the work that He has for us to do.

OUR COMMON BLESSINGS
(Lam. 3: 22-25)

In order to make the Scripture lesson clearer to the pupils, write on the blackboard some words that are synonymous with loving-kindness and compassion, such as "brotherly love," "kind-heartedness," "tenderness," "mercy," etc.

Have one of the pupils tell how he is merciful to his dog, also one of the girls how she shows loving-kindness to her bird.

Let the pupils name different ways of being merciful and of passing on the common blessings.

Make it a point to simplify the thought of the lesson by using illustrations from every-day life.

After the pupils have named ways in which we can be merciful to those about us and to our animal friends show that God is infinitely more merciful to us.

Outline a pitcher on the blackboard, and ask the pupils to tell what the expression "milk of human kindness" means. As they name different things that it stands for, write the words on the mouth of the pitcher.

In using the following acrostic print the word "merciful" with the letters arranged vertically instead of horizontally, and let the pupils complete the acrostic. The result will be something like this:

M indful
E very day
R ighteous
C ompassionate
I n His name
F orgiving
U nfailing
L ove

HOW TO GET A NEW HEART
(Ezek. 36: 25–27)

Take to the meeting for an object-lesson two of each of the following articles, one new and the other old: pocket-knife, books, shoes, or any other similar articles, as many as may be convenient.

Open the lesson talk by asking the pupils which they would rather have, a new thing or an old one. They will tell you the new. Here show the objects.

Ask how we get the new things. They will tell you that we buy them. Then ask how we can get new hearts. Who can furnish them? Does God sell them?

Have one of the pupils read Ezek. 36: 26.

Impress the thought that all may have new hearts just for the taking. We may have an old, distorted, sinful heart, which God will take away that He may give us a new, clean one in its place. Jesus said, "Ask, and ye shall receive."

Shall we not take this gift that is given so lovingly and freely?

With bowed heads let each of the pupils repeat David's prayer, "Create in me a clean heart, O God; and renew a right spirit within me."

HOW ONE BOY SHOWED HIS COLORS
(Dan. 6: 10-23)

Previous to the meeting arrange with four or five of your pupils to tell some of the Bible stories of Daniel at the meeting; for instance, let one tell the story of his abstinence from meat and drink as found in Dan. 1; another, the story of his interpreting the king's dream, as found in the fourth chapter of Daniel; another, the story of Daniel in the lions' den, found in the sixth chapter of Daniel.

As the story of our lesson is told, sketch a window on the blackboard. Ask the pupils to tell you what to name the window. Lead them to tell you, "Prayer." Write the name over the window. Draw from the pupils the lesson that each of us should have a window in our hearts, which looks toward the city of God. Draw a heart around the window. This window in our hearts is prayer. But before we can have this window of prayer we must have faith. Get a definition of faith. Lead the pupils to study Daniel's faith as one after another of the stories is told. Daniel had faith to believe God would hear his prayer, and this gave him courage. We can get courage to do right in the same way in which Daniel got it.

The story is told of how a soldier in the Northern army was sent South as a spy. Now, when a soldier is acting as a spy, he has to be very careful and keep out of sight of the enemy, or he will be either shot or captured.

Night came on, and the soldier knew he was among the enemy. He felt that every move he made might betray him into their hands. So he cautiously crept into a thicket, and lay down near a log. He felt all alone with not a friend near him. He could hear the movements of an army about him, and was sure the enemy were closing in on him. After many long hours dawn came, then the light of day; and, as the soldier cautiously raised his head to see the army of the enemy, behold! there stood line after line of the Union soldiers, his own army of the North. They, not the enemy, had surrounded him in the night. Just so with us. When we feel all alone, as Daniel did, if we but look around us, through the eyes of faith, we shall see a host of friends, and God, who is always on the side of those who have courage to do right.

A LIONS' DEN
(DAN. 6: 19-23)

Let the story of Daniel in the lions' den be told by the committee that has this lesson in charge. Arrange for one of the pupils to be prepared to tell what kind of king Darius was. Of what country was he king, and what people did he rule? Who were his captives?

Review the incidents of Daniel's life. For what reason was he thrown into the lions' den?

Who was the happier that night, the king in his richly appointed bed, or Daniel in the den of lions?

Why was Daniel the happier?

What was the effect of Daniel's faith?

Can we have the same kind of faith?

Draw a crown with a brace after it, also an angel's wing and a brace. Write in the brace with the crown a brief story, or words that will indicate the kind of people Daniel lived among, what they worshipped, what kind of king held him captive; and in the brace with the wing write some words that will tell the story of Daniel's life and purposes.

Lead the pupils to see that we often meet "lions."

Sometimes we may be thrust among them as Daniel was. Teach the lesson that our "lions" are the sins that we meet day by day. Sometimes we meet them willingly, but other times we are cast among them; but, if we use Daniel's weapons, prayer and faith, these lions will not hurt us.

SHORT-LIVED GOODNESS
(Hos. 6:4)

Combine with the Scripture reading Matt. 13: 5-7. This will illustrate more clearly the topic of "Short-lived Goodness."

Ask the pupils whether they ever pretended to be good when in reality they had been naughty. Also ask whether they have ever known people whose outside life seemed good and righteous while at heart they were deceitful and treacherous.

Write the word "Deserter" on the blackboard, and tell the story of soldiers who deserted just at the time when they were needed most. They liked the uniform, the marching, and the band; but they did not like to fight; so the night before the battle they would sneak out and get away.

It is just so with some Christians. They like to dress up nicely, and go to church, and be in some elaborate entertainment; but, when it comes to real Christian service, they always have some excuse.

Now imagine that we are some kind of seed, and are going to be planted in the ground. Should we rather be planted in the rich soil, and grow strong day by day and year by year, or in the "rocky soil," where we should spring up when the sun comes out, and flourish for a little while, then droop and die?

Write the word "Faithful" on the blackboard. Draw a brace after it, and let the pupils name Bible characters who have been faithful. Also draw a brace after the word "deserter," and fill it with Bible characters who have displayed "short-lived goodness."

Deserter { Cain, Esau, Jonah, Judas

Faithful { Moses, Abraham, David, Daniel, Paul

Which shall we be like when we grow to manhood and womanhood?

A MAN WHO SHIRKED
(Jonah 1: 1–3)

Make a chalk-talk of this lesson. In advance arrange with one of the boys to tell the story of Jonah as given in the first chapter. As the story is being told, outline a map which will show the location of the places mentioned in the lesson. Also draw a ship on the Mediterranean Sea to represent the journey which Jonah made.

Place emphasis on Jonah's running away from his duty, and trying to escape from the presence of God.

Sketch some boys and girls on the blackboard. Draw a brace on each side of these, and over the left-hand brace write, "Boys and girls who shirk"; over the right-hand brace, "Boys and girls who are true." Then have the pupils fill the braces with words that tell what kind of boys and girls shirk and what kind are true. Beneath these write the words "Remedy for shirking," and draw a brace after it. Then let the pupils tell what will help a person who has been in the habit of shirking.

THE LAST JOURNEY IN THE OLD TESTAMENT
(MAL. 4: 1-6)

After the Scripture lesson has been read call special attention to the fifth and sixth verses. Then have Matt. 11: 11-14 and Luke 1: 17 read.

Make clear to the pupils that the prophecy of Malachi has reference to John the Baptist, as the two references in the New Testament show us.

Draw from the pupils the story of John the Baptist. Have one of them read John 1: 6-8, 23.

Show that John was sent by God to tell the people that Christ was coming. Illustrate this by the advance agents of our big shows. They tell the people by the big bills they paste up on the boards that something grand and wonderful is coming. So John the Baptist was sent by God to tell every one that some one grand and wonderful, some one that would be a Saviour for all the world, was coming.

It would be well to let the message of the New Testament enter into this lesson. Have the pupils tell the story of the Christ-child, and by a few well-chosen questions bring out the story of His life and the great purpose of His coming.

Write in bold letters on the blackboard, "For God so loved the world, that he gave his only begotten Son, that whosoever believeth on him should not perish, but have eternal life."

PART TWO
NEW TESTAMENT STORIES

NEW TESTAMENT
WHAT THE WISE MEN FOUND

A wonderful thing happened this first Christmas. Up to this time there had been a kind and loving Father who had made the world, and created man, and many other things, all of which showed much loving thought and planning. Not only did He give us food, clothes, homes, and many other needful things, but beautiful flowers, rocks, music, birds, etc., to enjoy.

After He had given us all of these things He saw that there was another greater want than any He had given us. We needed a Saviour.

Have the class repeat John 3: 16.

Have one pupil tell of Joseph and Mary stopping at the inn, and being put into a stable to sleep.

Another pupil may tell of the visit of the wise men. Help to emphasize the thought that they found the Saviour of the world, that the little Babe in the manger was the Redeemer of the world, that while the wise men were among the first to find Him, we must all find Him, and love and worship Him just as they did.

SUGGESTIONS. This lesson should be selected as a Christmas lesson.

The idea of why we give Christmas presents should be carefully explained.

A week previous the children may be asked each to bring a gift to the class or meeting. Urge that they be *real* gifts, not just something that they do not care for. A small Christmas tree can be trimmed with these, and the pupils present it to a poor family, who will not be apt to have a very merry Christmas.

Or a Christmas box can be planned, and sent to some unfortunate children, to a children's hospital, or refuge.

THE BOY JESUS
(Luke 2: 45-50)

Arrange a meeting with one of your committees, and prepare the following object-lesson:

Secure a piece of pasteboard or a wooden board about two feet square. Cover this with gold or silver paper; or, if this is not to be had, black cloth will answer. Outline on this a large cross, and in the centre of it mount a picture of Christ. Take this and a bottle of paste to the class.

In your opening talk tell the pupils that we are going to have a new pupil join our class to-day. He wants to become one of us, and stay all the year, and longer if we will let Him. Here show the picture mounted on the board, and ask the pupils whether they know who this is that wants to join our class. Here a vote may be taken whether they will admit Him or not.

After the lesson story has been read, draw from the pupils all the incidents in Christ's life up to this time: His birth, the visit of the wise men, the flight into Egypt, His home in Nazareth, etc. Bring out clearly that Jesus was about His Father's business, also the lesson of His quick obedience to His parents when they found Him. Make clear also that His return to Nazareth with His parents meant eighteen years of seclusion and work, but that these years were the preparation for His great ministry and a gaining of strength to bear the sins of the world and to die on the cross.

CHRIST CHOOSING HIS HELPERS
(JOHN 1: 35-45)

Have one of the older pupils who can draw well prepare the following object-lesson, which will not only be useful for this lesson, but will be a help throughout the year, and if carefully prepared can be hung in the room and referred to at any time during the year's work. On a piece of white cardboard or heavy white paper about eighteen inches square outline a wheel with twelve spokes. The centre or hub of the wheel should contain a cross, which will represent Christ. Around the tire write the word "World," and write the apostles' names on the spokes. This will represent the twelve apostles centred in Christ and reaching out into the world.

On a previous Sunday tell the pupils to find out all they can about the twelve apostles; to study the characteristics of each and his particular relation to Christ; and to learn what trades they followed, what they gave up in order to follow Christ, etc.

Let this lesson be a character-study of the apostles.

Make it so plain to the pupils that they will feel acquainted with these men when the lesson is over.

Teach the lesson that, if we would bring others to Jesus, we must do just as the apostles did, and tell our relatives and friends about Jesus. The first and most important thing is that we must follow Jesus ourselves, and those about us will see Jesus in our lives and know that we have been with Him.

An object-lesson may be used that will be very pleasing to the pupils. Place one common-sized candle in a candlestick, and have four small Christmas candles of different colors; these may be made to stand up by taking for each a piece of cardboard two inches square, warming the lower end of the candle over a flame, and holding it against the centre of the cardboard until the wax cools. Light the large candle, which will represent Christ. Take two of the little candles in your hands; one we will call Andrew; the other, Peter; now light the one we call Andrew from the larger candle; then with it light the one we call Peter; then treat the other two small candles in the same way, calling one Philip and the other Nathanael. This will show to the pupils how we can keep taking God's light to others, and in that way the whole world may become light with God's love.

A BEAUTIFUL WELL
(John 4: 5-10)

Have in readiness a sand-board filled with moist sand, some evergreen branches, a few cut flowers, a number of small stones, a tiny bucket with cord attached (this may be made of brown paper), a small glass, a small cup, and a cross about three inches high.

I think the lessons more effective when the work of arranging the sand-board is performed by the pupils, guided, of course, by the teacher.

In arranging the sand-board first sink the cup in the sand, and let it be filled about half full of water. Upon this let the small stones be piled to make the curb. This will represent Jacob's well. Then the branches and flowers may be stuck into the sand in an attractive manner. While this is being done, let the lesson talk bring out the story of how Jesus, being tired with His long journey, stopped at Jacob's well for a drink of water. How refreshing it must have been! for in that climate the sand is very hot, and one gets more fatigued in walking than one does in our own land. Here place the small cross beside the well. This will represent Christ at the well. Also fill the glass with water, and lead the pupils to tell how necessary water is to our life, that we could not live without it. Then speak of the water of life, and lead the children to see how it is just as necessary to our spiritual life as water is to our physical life.

Away in the upper peninsula of Michigan lives a very dear old lady. She is bent and crippled with rheumatism, and has to walk with a cane. Now in that section of the country there are very few churches, and many people never hear about Jesus; and the little children have no Sunday-school where they may go and learn about Him. Grandmother McKinney loves Jesus. There is no church near her home; but some distance away there is a schoolhouse, and once in a long time some good man goes there and preaches about Jesus. To get to the schoolhouse Grandmother McKinney has to go down a steep hill, cross a ravine, and climb a hill on the other side; but she loves so much to hear about her dear Master that she slowly and painfully travels that difficult road to and from the schoolhouse.

It grieved her heart very much to feel that there were so many people in our land that did not know of Jesus; so she began to plan how she could help to send some one to preach the gospel to these people. What could she do? She could not get away from home, and she had no money to give; so "she did what she could"; she pieced a quilt, sat and toiled day after day with her dim eyes and crippled hands till she had it finished. Then one day, when one of those good missionaries who "go about doing good" came to Grandmother McKinney's house, she gave him the quilt and told him to sell it for what he could get, and give the money to the home-missionary society.

May we not learn a beautiful lesson from Grandmother McKinney?

CHRIST AND THE NOBLEMAN'S SON
(JOHN 4: 46-53)

Draw a heart at the right side of the blackboard and a cross at the left side. Draw a line between them. The heart represents the nobleman's son, who was sick at Capernaum. The cross represents Christ, and the line a wireless telegraph.

Here have the story of the nobleman's son told by the pupils. Christ was in another place, so He could not go and see this boy just then, but he sent a message of love and healing. Here make clear to the pupils how it is not necessary for Christ to be visibly present, that this message of love and healing can get to any one just as it went to this nobleman's son.

Have the pupils tell what a miracle is. Make clear to them why Christ used miracles, and use verse 48 and the truth that Christ is ever present and ready if we will but go to Him and ask for help as did this nobleman.

Arrange with your flower committee to meet with you during the week. Let the members make some small envelopes. You will need as many envelopes as you have pupils. Put into each envelope some seed. It is not material what kind of seed is used; wheat, corn, beans, or different kinds of flower-seeds may be used. After the seeds have been put into the envelopes seal them. On each envelope write "Faith Seeds."

Pass the envelopes of seeds. Tell the pupils these are "faith seeds." Ask them why they are, and lead them to see that the fact that we plant the seeds in the ground shows we have faith and believe they will grow. Tell them to take the seeds home, and sometime during the week plant them in a box and set the box in a window; to water and care for them, and bring them to the class at Easter. Then we will finish our lesson on "Faith Seeds."

CHRIST'S BEATITUDES
(MATT. 5: 1-12)

Have one of your committees meet with you and make for an object-lesson and gift some little cardboard pitchers. These will be very pretty if made of tinted cardboard.

They are to represent the bottle of precious ointment that Mary poured on Jesus' feet.

On each pitcher have one of the Beatitudes neatly written. A tiny ribbon may be tied in the handle or around the neck of the pitcher. These will look very pretty if pinned to a large sheet of pasteboard and hung in the front of the classroom.

Number the pupils one, two, three, four, etc., and place the numbers on the blackboard far enough apart to make a small brace after each.

Ask each pupil, beginning at number one, to rise and repeat the Beatitude he likes best. Write a part of the Beatitude in the brace, and sum up in a word or two the reason why he likes that Beatitude, and place it under the Beatitude, somewhat as follows:

1. Blessed are the pure in heart —
   If I keep my heart pure, I can see God.
2. Blessed are the peace-makers —
   It is right to make peace.
3. Blessed are the meek —
   "Meek" means "gentle."

After each pupil has taken part in this way let the little cardboard pitchers be passed, after which ask that all heads be bowed, and ask God to help them remember the promise of each Beatitude.

A "SHINE-OUT" LESSON
(MATT. 5: 13-16)

Have for an object-lesson some salt, some white sand or powdered chalk, a candle, a half-bushel measure or a box, and two glasses of water.

A very pretty gift to accompany this lesson would be a card with a candle outlined, and the Scripture reference, Matt. 5: 13-16, printed neatly on it. Prepare one for each pupil.

A suggested object-talk:

Pupils, I have in these dishes two kinds of material that seem to be very much alike. I will pass them among you and ask you to feel them, but not taste them. Now I will ask Mary to read the first verse of our Scripture lesson. I will put these materials into the two glasses of water, and we shall see whether they taste differently. You tell me one is salt; now, what is the other? Does it taste like salt? It does not. Then we shall call it salt that has lost its savor. That is, it has lost its taste; and, if mother was cooking our dinner, and should put in some of this (holding up the glass with the sand in it), would the dinner taste good? No, indeed; we could scarcely eat it. But, if she put in some of the real salt, it would make our dinner good.

Now can you tell me what Christ meant when He called us the salt of the earth? (Draw out the meaning of the text, so that the children may see that, as salt makes our food good, so we should make the world good. Have your candle lighted under the box, or light it in such a way that the pupils will not see it.)

Now, pupils, I have a candle in this room; do you see it anywhere? Does it make the room any lighter? Why not? Robert may read the fourteenth and fifteenth verses of our lesson. (As these are being read, uncover the candle, and set it where all can see the light.)

Now let us read the sixteenth verse together. Christ is the light of the world, and He says we may also be the light of the world, if we will but let our candles shine, and not hide them.

How many of us want to shine out for Jesus? (Ask the pupils to name ways in which boys and girls may shine for Jesus.) Now let every head be bowed and every eye closed, and let every one of us ask Jesus to help us to be the "light of the world" and the "salt of the earth."

THE KIND OF PRAYING JESUS LIKES
(MATT. 6: 7-13; 7: 11)

Write the subject of the lesson near the top of the blackboard. After the first Scripture reference is read make a brace on the blackboard, and write the word "How" in front of it. Then draw from the pupils the different teachings of the Lord's Prayer. It may work out somewhat like the following:

HOW
- To address God
- To pray for His kingdom to come
- To ask for our daily food
- To ask Him to forgive us and to help us to forgive others
- To keep us from temptation
- To rescue us from evil

The next Scripture reference tells us why we are to ask. Have this read, and make another brace with the word "Why" before it.

WHY
1. We must ask God if we want Him to give us things.
2. We must seek God if we hope to keep near Him.
   If we seek, we shall find.
3. We must knock at God's door if we want Him to open to us.
   "Knock, and it shall be opened unto you."

A third reference is 1 Thess. 5:17. This passage tells us when to pray.

Have two or three of the older pupils study the subject of wireless telegraphy. This should be arranged for on a previous Sunday. Also have one of the boys make two telephone-poles, about eighteen inches high, with the lower ends fastened into a board so that they will stand upright. These poles will represent the signal-stations of wireless telegraphy. On the top of one hang a card with the word "God" on it, and on the other a card with the word "Ourselves."

After the wireless telegraphy has been explained and talked over by the pupils apply it to the lesson, and show how prayer is talking to God; and just as the operator in wireless telegraphy believes his message will be received, so we must believe that God hears us when we pray. If man is able to establish connection between two distant points, may we not believe that God in His infinite power can establish connection between ourselves and Him?

THE SABBATH DAY

(LUKE 4: 16-22)

Write or print near the top of the blackboard the words, "Jesus went to church." Under this draw two long braces. Before one of them write the words "What to Do on Sunday," and in front of the other, "What Not to Do on Sunday."

Have the pupils name things that are right to do on the Sabbath and things that are not right to do on the Sabbath. As these are named, write them in the proper brace. It will work out somewhat as follows:

What to Do on Sunday
- Go to church
- Go to Sunday-school
- Go to Junior meeting
- Read the Bible
- Read good books
- Sing good songs
- Be happy
- Make others happy

What Not to Do on Sunday
- Be lazy
- Go to ball games
- Go visiting for pleasure
- Go on excursions
- Loaf about
- Have a feast

FOUR KINDS OF PEOPLE
(Mark 4: 14-20)

Have a pupil read, or, better still, tell in his own words, the story of the sower who went out to sow the seed, as the story is found in Mark 4: 3-9. As he tells the story, sketch figures to represent the highway, stony places, thorns, and fertile soil. After each of these draw a brace. If possible, use different-colored chalk for each of these pictures. After the pupil finishes telling the story lead the children to talk about the lesson text, apply it to each place where the seed fell, and bring out the thought that Christ meant to teach about each. Be sure in this lesson, as in all others, to let the pupils do the work, and just as far as possible use their own words in filling in the braces.

Wayside { Trampled down by sin
Carried away by pleasures

Stony Ground { Choked by anxiety, cares, worries, pleasures, and sins

Thorns { Ready to promise, but fails to do things
Changeable, unreliable

Good Ground { Those who love God and take care of the precious seed He sows in their hearts

JESUS FEEDS THE HUNGRY
(MARK 6: 35-44)

Prepare the sand-board as follows:

Heap the moist sand up so that it will represent a hillside. Stick some branches of trees around the sides and near the top of this. Flowers and moss may also be used to beautify it and give it a landscape effect. Have pebbles or sticks placed close together to represent the people. These should almost cover the hillside. Near the foot of the hill place a small cross to represent Christ.

Have one of your committees make twelve little baskets similar to May baskets which almost every child knows how to make; also bring some small pieces of bread to represent the fishes used by Christ in this miracle.

Let the lesson be read and thoroughly talked over by the pupils. Draw out all the incidents and facts regarding the multitude of people who had followed Christ around the lake. It had been a long, tiresome journey; and the people were weary and hungry. There seemed to be no way to feed them.

There was not sufficient food in this section of the country, and Christ saw that it was He alone that could feed them; so He performed this wonderful miracle, not only that they should have their physical hunger satisfied, but that He might show the glory of God and His divine power to this great multitude of people.

After the lesson thoughts have been discussed lead the pupils to make the application by having them name the good things that God is always giving us. These may be written on the blackboard as named. Lead the children to see that as twelve basketfuls were left after feeding the multitude, so God always gives us more than enough.

What should we do with what is left over?

How may we help to feed the hungry?

Should we ever be wasteful?

Can we always depend on God to supply our needs?

After the lesson is ended the twelve baskets may be filled with flowers and sent to the hospital, or be taken to sick and aged people.

A LESSON IN FORGIVENESS
(MATT. 18: 21, 22)

Arrange a meeting with one of your committees during a previous week, and have them make a number of small cardboard crosses. These should be quite tiny, not more than an inch long. On each one print or write a Bible reference. Those given in the daily Bible readings may be used. Also plan with the committee to bring a number of small bouquets to the meeting. There should be enough bouquets and crosses for each pupil to be provided with one. Place a cross in the centre of each bouquet of flowers, and arrange the bouquets in a pretty mound on a table in the classroom.

After the lesson has been read let it be carefully talked over, and bring out just what Christ meant by forgiving seventy times seven. Lead the pupils to see that He used this expression simply to show that we are always to forgive, that there are no limitations on our forgiveness. Call attention to the sentence in the Lord's Prayer that says, "Forgive us our debts as we forgive our debtors," and show that this means that just as we forgive people, so God will forgive us.

Show to the pupils that it is just as easy to excuse an offence as it is always to be finding fault.

Distribute the bouquets, and let each pupil find and read the reference that is written on the cross hidden among his flowers. Each pupil may keep his flowers, or they may be sent to a hospital or to some sick and shut-in person.

JESUS IN OUR HOMES
(Luke 10: 38-42; John 11: 5)

We shall make a chalk-talk of this lesson. Sketch a house on the blackboard in such a manner that the different rooms will show, and write the name of each room, such as "Library," "Dining-room," "Guest-room," etc.

Lead the pupils to tell how we may make Christ welcome in our homes. After this has been thoroughly talked over, ask in what way we can make Him an inmate of our library or living-room. Draw braces in the rooms, and, as the pupils suggest ways of welcoming Christ in the different rooms in our home, write the suggestions in their appropriate braces. For instance:

Library $\begin{cases} \text{Have only good books there} \\ \text{Make a place for the Bible on the library table} \\ \text{Have family worship} \end{cases}$

Dining-room $\begin{cases} \text{Return thanks for food} \\ \text{Eat in moderation} \end{cases}$

Guest-room $\begin{cases} \quad\quad\quad\quad \textit{Motto} \\ \text{"Christ is the unseen guest in this home."} \end{cases}$

Bedroom $\begin{cases} \text{Pray night and morning} \\ \text{Trust God in the darkness} \end{cases}$

Other rooms may be added if you see fit. The pupils will no doubt have appropriate suggestions ready for each room.

Now draw a heart on the blackboard. Ask a Junior to read Rev. 3:20. Point out that Jesus comes to our hearts and we can take Him into our homes when we have Him in our hearts.

Ask the Juniors to tell how He knocks at the heart's door. By His word, by the preaching of His servants, by conscience, which tells us to let Him in.

If you can get a picture showing Christ at the door, show it to the Juniors, and point out that the door has no outside latch. *We must open it from the inside.*

OUR NEIGHBORS
(LUKE 10: 25-37)

In giving this chalk-talk draw the pictures while you are telling the story. There will be no criticisms if they are imperfect. Our pupils are not critics, and these chalk-talks or picture stories are, I believe, enjoyed and appreciated more than anything else.

A Parable

Many years ago, near the Dead Sea, (can you tell me where that is?) there was a place named Jericho. Leading from this town to Jerusalem was a desolate, rocky, mountainous road. (Draw some mountains. This can be done by using the side of a short piece of chalk and making a few strokes upward on each side of the road or passage.) Robbers used to hide along this road, and attack people that passed by.

One day a certain man had to travel this road; and, as he was going along, some thieves came out and took all he had, his clothes and money, and beat him until he was nearly dead. Then they left him there in the road. (Draw the man in the road.)

Now in a little while a priest (who were the priests?) came along. He saw this poor man lying there suffering, but he did not go near. He probably was afraid of the robbers, or was so full of himself that he had no room in his heart for any one else. So he stepped over to the other side of the road, and went on. (Draw a small, narrow heart to represent the priest, and write the word "Self" in it.)

After a time Mr. Levite, a man who prided himself on being very good, came along. He stopped and looked at the helpless man, and probably thought, "I don't know this man; he is not my friend, and I have no time to bother with him"; so he passed on. (Represent the Levite in the same way as the priest.)

Now it happened that a Samaritan (have the pupils tell something about the Samaritans) was passing along this road, and he came to the place where the man lay. (Draw a large heart in the road. It should be large enough to take in the figure representing the man.) He stooped over him, and his heart was touched. He just set about helping that poor man. He took some cloth he had, and some oil and wine, which were used then for pouring on wounds; then he helped the wounded man upon his own horse, and went slowly and tenderly to an inn. (Draw an inn.) He gave the innkeeper some money, and told him to take good care of this man, and that when he returned he would pay whatever more was right.

After the story has been told ask each pupil to tell what lesson he has learned from it. Teach the following verse: "Thou shalt love the Lord thy God with all thy heart, and with all thy soul, and with all thy strength, and with all thy mind; and thy neighbor as thyself."

JESUS, THE GOOD SHEPHERD
(John 10: 11-16)

After the lesson is read have the pupils tell you the qualities of a good shepherd. As points are suggested, have some of the pupils who have been supplied with slips with just the verse or part of a verse written out, read or repeat the text that tells about that particular quality. The following questions and their answers will give the idea:

Where will a good shepherd enter in? "But he that entereth in by the door is the shepherd of the sheep."

How does he call his sheep? "The sheep hear his voice, and he calleth his own sheep by name."

Does he drive them out? He "leadeth them out." "He goeth before them, and the sheep follow him."

What would happen if a stranger should try to get the sheep out in the same way? "A stranger will they not follow, but will flee from him; for they know not the voice of strangers."

What is the difference between the good shepherd and a hireling? "The hirelong fleeth, because he is an hireling, and careth not for the sheep." "The good shepherd giveth his life for his sheep."

What care does the good shepherd have for other sheep besides his own flock? "Other sheep I have, which are not of this fold; them also I must bring; and they shall hear my voice, and there shall be one fold and one shepherd."

A number of other qualities may be brought out by appropriate questions.

Who are the sheep?	People who need God's care Everybody
Why do the sheep know the true shepherd?	He loves them He cares for them He seeks them He tends them
How may we be His lambs?	Love Him Follow Him Obey Him
Who is the wolf?	Satan All who are enemies of God
Why should the sheep fear the wolf?	He will destroy them Scatter them from the fold, etc.
How may the lambs be saved?	Keep close to the shepherd Stay near the shelter of the fold Not follow other voices

THE CHILDREN'S HOSANNAS
(Matt. 21:15, 16)

Lead the pupils to tell what they think it means for children to praise Jesus.

Number the pupils, and let each one take the verse in the One Hundred and Forty-fifth Psalm that corresponds to his number. If there are more pupils than verses, two or more may take the same verse.

Make a large brace on the blackboard, and in front of it write the words "How to Praise God."

Now the pupils, with their Bibles, may find ways to praise God. Ask number one to rise, read his verse, and tell how it says God may be praised. It may be summed up in the following or a similar sentence; "Bless His name forever." Write this in the brace.

Number two may rise, read his verse, and tell how it says we should praise God, and so proceed until all the verses have been read. If two have the same number, let them both rise, let one read the verse, and let the other tell the lesson it brings to us.

The following brace is suggestive. Use the thoughts of the pupils as far as possible.

How to Praise God:
1. Bless His name forever.
2. Praise Him every day.
3. Praise Him because He is great.
4. Praise Him to one another.
5. Speak of His glory, honor, majesty, and works.
6. Declare His greatness.
7. Sing praises unto God.
8. Praise Him because He is full of love and merciful.
9. Praise Him because He is good.
10. Let our works praise Him.
11. Speak of His kingdom.
12. Make known to others His acts.
13. Tell others of God's eternal kingdom.
14. Tell others that He helps and comforts.
15. Praise Him for providing for us.
16. Praise Him for satisfying us.
17. Praise Him for His goodness.
18. Praise Him for hearing our prayers.
19. Praise Him for answering our prayers.
20. Praise Him for saving the good.
21. Our mouths should praise God forever.

The blackboard exercises should be interspersed with verses of songs so as not to get tiresome.

THE GREATEST COMMANDMENT
(MATT. 22: 35-40)

Draw a brace on the blackboard, and before it write the words "Ten Commandments." Ask the pupils to repeat the Ten Commandments; and, as each one is repeated, condense it and write in the brace. After this draw another brace, and in this write, "Matt. 22: 37." If there is room, write the words instead of the reference. Enclose the word "and" between two small braces; then write the second commandment or the reference to it, Matt. 22: 39. This will work out somewhat as follows:

$$\text{Ten Commandments} \begin{cases} 1. \ldots \\ 2. \ldots \\ 3. \ldots \\ 4. \ldots \\ 5. \ldots \\ 6. \ldots \\ 7. \ldots \\ 8. \ldots \\ 9. \ldots \\ 10. \ldots \end{cases} \text{Matt. 22: 37 and Matt. 22: 39}$$

Lead the pupils to tell the story of the Ten Commandments, who gave them, to whom they were given, when they were given, etc. After these points have been carefully talked over, call attention to the lesson text. Carefully explain what Christ meant to teach by this, and lead the pupils to see that these commandments include all the others, and that, if the greatest commandment is fulfilled, all the Ten Commandments will be kept.

How can we live the greatest commandment?

What kind of world would this be if all lived it?

OUR TALENTS
(MATT. 25: 14-30)

Arrange for this lesson on a preceding Sunday. Ask each pupil to bring to the class from six to one dozen nice potatoes. Also provide a bushel-basket to put them in. These can be used as a thank-offering for the benefit of the needy. Also bring two cents to the class, one old and dull, the other bright and shiny. Tell a story something like the following to illustrate the lesson of the talents:

Once upon a time there were two boys who were great chums. The one boy's name was Joe, and the other's Carl. One day the boys were sitting on the edge of the sidewalk, looking over the things that they had in their pockets. You can well imagine something of the assortment if you have ever been acquainted with a boy. There were nails and screws, jack-knives and marbles, top-strings and fish-hooks galore. Pretty soon Joe fished a little deeper into one of his pockets, and drew out an old, rusty-looking cent. (Here show the dull cent.)

"Hello, Carl, what do you think? I found a penny."

"O, that's nothing," replied Carl. "I have more money than that. Uncle John was at our house the other day, and gave me a quarter. I spent most of it, though"; and Carl pulled out a five-cent piece and a bright cent. (Here show the new cent.)

"Let's go down to Hank Miller's, and buy some gum with these cents," said Carl.

"Can't do it," replied Joe. "I've got to go out to Farmer Brown's, and get my father some seed-potatoes. I don't think I'll spend my cent for gum, anyway."

Now Carl went down to the grocery-store, but the new cent looked very good to him; so he thought he would not spend it; but instead he spent his five cents for gum. Then he took the tin-foil off the gum, and wrapped his new cent carefully in it. When he got home, he put it away in a drawer with some keepsakes he had.

When Joe got out to Mr. Brown's, he found the farmer planting potatoes, and was very much interested in the proceeding. Mr. Brown told him how he cut the eyes out of the potatoes for seed, how deep and how far apart to plant them, how many times he hoed them throughout the season, until Joe thought he would like to try it for himself. So, when the farmer had filled his basket with seed-potatoes, Joe said, "Mr. Brown, I have a cent I would like to invest in a potato."

The farmer smiled a little as he picked out the largest potato he could find in the bin, and Joe went home very happy, planning his potato-patch. He counted the eyes in that potato ten times before he reached home. The potato had eight eyes, and Joe figured that, according to what Farmer Brown said, he could plant four hills of potatoes if he cut the eyes out in the proper way.

Now it would take too long to tell how many times Joe hoed and watered his potato-patch; but one day late in the fall he was very busy, and Carl did not see much of him until about five o'clock in the evening. Then he saw Joe going down the street with a wheelbarrow.

"Hello, Joe, what you got there?"

"Potatoes," replied Joe.

Carl became interested at once, and Joe told his story of how he had bought a potato of Farmer Brown with his dull cent, and now he was going to market with a lot of as fine potatoes as you ever saw.

"Why, Joe, you will get fifty cents at least for those potatoes," said Carl. "I wish I had bought potatoes with my cent and started a garden. I've got it all wrapped up at home, and put away in a drawer; and it is still a cent. You used yours, and now have fifty cents instead of one cent. I tell you I am not going to leave that cent there any longer, for I believe there is a better use for money than keeping it hidden away."

"Right you are," said Joe as he trundled his wheelbarrow along.

SPRING FLOWERS AND THE RISEN CHRIST

(MATT. 28: 1-8)

Have the following exercise carried out by four of the pupils:

I.

A child will come forward with a bulb in his hand and say:

> I hold in my hand a little dried-up bulb. They tell me that within it is *life*. I cannot see how this can be, for there is neither root nor stalk. Just these brown, dry husks. Surely no life can come from this!

II.

A child comes forward with a cross. This may be made of slender sticks wound with white cotton batting.

> I had a Friend whose "life was the light of men"; but He was crucified on the cross, and they buried Him in a tomb, and sealed it with a great stone. They tell me He will come forth out of the tomb, but I do not see how this can be.

III.

A child will come forward with an Easter lily. If possible, have a potted plant for this.

> I hold in my hand a lily, pure, spotless, and fragrant. A short time ago it was a dry bulb, which we buried in the earth. It burst forth in all this beauty. This is resurrection.

IV.

A child will come forward with a crown in his hand, which he will raise and place on his head as he speaks the last sentence.

> The angels broke the seal and rolled the stone away, and Christ came forth, a King. This is resurrection. We too may rise, and wear the crown of rejoicing that fadeth not away.

It would be very well to have the four pupils who take part in this sing a simple Easter song at the close of the exercise.

The following recitation may be used:

> *O Earth, throughout thy borders*
>   *Re-don thy fairest dress;*
> *And everywhere, O Nature,*
>   *Throb with new happiness;*
> *Once more to new creation*
>   *Awake, and death gainsay,*
> *For death is swallowed up of life,*
>   *And Christ is risen to-day!*
>
> *Let peals of jubilation*
>   *Ring out in all the lands;*
> *With hearts of deep elation*
>   *Let sea with sea clasp hands;*
> *Let one supreme Te Deum*
>   *Roll round the world's highway,*
> *For death is swallowed up of life,*
>   *And Christ is risen to-day!*
>
>   GEORGE NEWELL LOVEJOY

A SHIPWRECK
(ACTS 27: 9-44)

The Scripture lesson is too long to be read with profit to the pupils; so a good way would be to divide it into sections. Let one tell about the storm at sea, how Paul advised the sailors not to sail at that time, how the sailors ignored his words, etc. Have another tell about the visit of the angel to Paul, and its result; another, about the sailors' fear of being dashed on the rocks, their casting out anchors, and Paul's reassurance and faith; another may finish the story of their breaking their fast, and the other events that followed, closing with their escape to land on pieces of the wreck. Told in this way, the story will be very interesting.

The lessons from the story may be drawn from the pupils. They may be summed up as follows:

First. It is better to follow the advice of a wise God-fearing person than to go on blindly in our own way.

Second. If we trust God, the angels will not be very far away.

Third. Use the anchor of faith, or we shall be dashed upon the rocks of sin and perish.

Fourth. Take care of health, so that we may have strength to meet difficulties. Thank God for what He gives us.

Fifth. When the storm of life is fierce and its waves high, we may trust ourselves to God's care, and He will bring us safely to land.

A very pretty gift for this lesson would be an anchor cut from tinted cardboard, with the word "Faith" printed on it. Give one to each pupil at the close of the lesson.

The sentence prayers following will be a request to God for more faith.

So I go on not knowing; I would not if I might;
I'd rather walk in the dark with God than go alone in the light.
I'd rather walk with Him by faith than walk alone by sight.'

— MARY G. BRAINARD

HOW CHRIST WANTS US TO CARE FOR OUR BODIES
(ROM. 12:1)

The materials for the object-lesson are a vase, a pan of water, dry cloth, different kinds of weeds, some of which should be poisonous (care must be taken not to use any that are poisonous to touch) and some ill-smelling. Also procure some beautiful, sweet-smelling flowers, and some slips of paper on which are written the names of different kinds of sins that spoil our lives and of things that make our lives good and beautiful. Pin these slips on the weeds and the flowers. Make the outside of the vase look soiled and dirty. Fill the vase with the ill-smelling weeds, and you are ready to begin the lesson-talk.

The vase represents our bodies. What is the matter with the vase before us? Does it remind you of some boys and girls? Its beauty is all covered up and spoiled with dirt. I have seen boys and girls whose beauty was spoiled by being covered up with something that looks much like that which is spoiling the vase. Their finger-nails were edged with black; their hair was uncombed; their teeth needed brushing; and their clothes were soiled and untidy. Now, do you think there is any need that any boy or girl should go about like that? Pass the vase among the pupils, and ask them to examine and smell the contents. Explain that some of the weeds are poisonous, others ill-smelling and offensive, and others a perfect nuisance because they always crowd out the good plants. Take out the weeds one by one, and read the slip attached to each. The weeds represent the little sins that get into our hearts, spoil and poison them, and crowd out the good.

Now empty the vase, and wash it in the basin of water; then wipe it dry with the cloth. This illustrates how we may purify our bodies. Lead the pupils to tell how to be neat and tidy and how to take care of their bodies.

Put the flowers into the vase one by one. Read the slips which show the good and beautiful things that we should have in our hearts. Have the pupils name other ways in which we may consecrate our bodies. When the flowers are all in the vase, pass it among the pupils, and let them admire and smell them. The contrast between the first state of the vase and the last will make an enduring impression on the minds of the children.

Close with the beautiful hymn, "Take my life, and let it be," by Frances R. Havergal.

TALKING TO GOD
(EPH. 6: 18; GEN. 18: 16-33)

Bring to the class a letter, a telegram, and the picture of a telephone. Use these in the object-lesson to show the different means of communicating with friends.

Show the objects, and lead the pupils to discuss them. Ask whether there is any other way of communicating with God when we want to ask something.

Ask in what way Abraham communicated with God when he wanted to ask something.

Ask the pupils how they ask father or mother for something they want.

These suggestions will bring out the thought very forcibly that, when we want to tell God anything, we can use the easiest way of all. Just talk to Him.

Draw three braces on the blackboard. In front of one write the words "How Abraham Prayed," in front of another, "How Jesus Prayed," in front of the last, "How We Should Pray."

Have the braces filled, one at a time, in the order named. They will work out somewhat as follows:

How Abraham Prayed	Earnestly Simply Repeatedly As to a friend
How Jesus Prayed	As a child would ask his father When in trouble When He needed help Asked repeatedly Often
How We Should Pray	Ask for what we need Ask for help Often Believing Trusting

Urge this thought: We speak just to God, not to those present or to the teacher, but just to God, who is listening for little voices.

THE PRAYERS

"*I was in heaven one day when all the prayers*
Came in, and angels bore them up the stairs
    Unto a place where he
    Who was ordained such ministry
Should sort them so that in that palace bright
The presence-chamber might be duly dight;
For they were like to flowers of various bloom,
And a divinest fragrance filled the room.
Then did I see the great sorter choose
One flower that seemed to be a hedgeling rose,
    And from the tangled press

Of that irregular loveliness
Set it apart, and, 'This,' I heard him say,
'Is for the Master'; so upon his way
He would have passed; then I to him,
'Whence is this rose, O thou of cherubim
The chiefest?' 'Knowest thou not?' he said, and smiled;
'This is the first prayer of a little child.'"

MAKING THE BEST OF THINGS
(PHIL. 4: 4–7, 11, 12)

Write near the top of the blackboard the words, "MAKE THE BEST OF THINGS." Draw a brace; in front of it write, "What things?" Then have the pupils name things in our lives that we should make the best of. Write them in the brace as they are named.

In front of another brace write the word "How?" The pupils will suggest ways of making the best of things. Fill the brace as they answer.

It will work out somewhat as follows:

What Things? { Hard work
Hard lessons
Poor clothes
Unkindness in others
Giving up to others
Slights

How? { Prayer
Patience
Joyfulness
Smiles
Songs
Sacrifice
Kindness

You will find that your pupils will think of enough answers to these questions to fill large braces.

Lead the pupils to tell how Christ made the best of things. They will recall incidents of His life that will illustrate the topic.

Make the Best of It

If at dawn in the morning the rising-bell rings,
And you're sleepy, and hate to be bothered with things,
  Make the best of it.

If you come in too late and the coffee is cold,
If the meat and potatoes are soggy, don't scold;
  Make the best of it.

If your mother is baking, and calls for some wood,
When you want to play ball, skate, or coast, just be good;
  Make the best of it.

If an errand's to run, and you're called on to go
Just as Ned comes to help you build forts out of snow;
  Make the best of it.

If the world or the people should e'er use you ill,
If your work seems too hard, press right on, trust God, still;
  Make the best of it.

HOW TO KEEP SWEET
(Col. 3: 8–15)

The following is a suggested chalk-talk:

Pupils, I am going to make a garden to-day; and all must help me, or I fear the weeds will grow so fast that we shall not raise a good crop. Now all watch me while I make the fence. Will some one tell me why we put a high fence around the garden?

Yes, to keep out chickens, dogs, and other things which would destroy the seeds we have planted.

Will the fence keep out all the things that destroy a garden? Fred says it will not. Now, Fred, tell us what there are that the fence will not keep out.

"Weeds," did I hear you say? Now I am going to name this garden "our tempers," and O, such a lot of weeds are growing here! What shall we name the weeds in this garden? Angry words, unkind words, etc. What shall we do about the weeds?

Floyd, tell me what your father does when the weeds grow in his garden.

He gets a man to help hoe them out, does he? (Draw a hoe.)

Now we cannot get the weeds out of our garden alone; and, if we let them grow, they will soon crowd out everything else, and "our tempers" will just be full of angry words, sour looks, and spiteful replies. Whom can *we* get to help hoe out the weeds?

Jessie says, "Jesus will help us."

We will name the hoe "Bible," and bow our heads, and each one will ask Jesus to help us get sweet tempers.

Russell H. Conwell tells this story:

"My home was in the Berkshire Hills. One evening, tired out with the toil of the day, I thought to leave my children and walk up the hill to see the mountaineer.

"As I crossed the brook and started up the hillside, I heard the voice of my little child calling, 'Papa, hurry and catch up with the sunshine.'

"To please my little girl, I quickened my steps, and soon found my head in the sunlight while my feet were in the shadow. So on I went all the way up the hill with my head in the sunlight and my feet in the shadow, till all the glory of the Berkshire sunset burst on my vision."

The story brings us this lesson: We may keep our tempers sweet by keeping our heads in God's sunlight, even if we do walk in a world shadowed with sin; and by and by we shall see the glory of eternity burst on our vision.

A MISSIONARY LESSON
(2 Thess. 3:1)

Ask each member of the class to find out the name and residence of one missionary, and learn all he can about him and the work he is trying to do. Get a sheet of cardboard and cut it into cards about three by five inches in size.

The children should press some flowers, and paste them neatly on the cards, leaving room to write a pretty verse or a kind message, and a pupil's name. Autumn leaves may be used in place of the pressed flowers if you desire.

If possible, get a kodak picture of your class. If not, print the name of your class neatly on one card for the cover. Have two holes punched in one end of each card. You can get this done at a lawyer's office. Have each pupil write a greeting and his name on a card; then tie all the cards together with a fluffy bunch of baby ribbon.

This will form a pretty autograph album, and may be sent to a missionary. The familiar home flowers or leaves with the greetings will gladden a heart that longs for a sight of "home things."

Several of these albums may be made and sent to as many missionaries.

Have the missionary committee make a lot of penny banks, and give one to each pupil two or three weeks before this lesson. These should be made out of light-weight cardboard as follows: Cut a piece of cardboard three inches long and two and a quarter inches wide. Make a hole near one end of the short side large enough to put a cent through. Fasten the ends together with paste. Cut slits a quarter of an inch deep and an eighth of an inch apart all around both ends of the tube. Bend these in. Cut a round piece of cardboard the size of a quarter of a dollar for the top of the bank, and a piece an inch and a half square for the bottom. Paste these on the ends of the tube, taking care to put the round piece on the end that has the holes for putting the pennies through. Lay a little weight on top till it dries. If the ends are made of different-colored cardboard, the effect is very pleasing to the children.

One of these little banks will entice many pennies. If the end is torn, open carefully when the money is taken out; it can be pasted on and used again. These banks should be in charge of the missionary committee.

WHAT JESUS BORE FOR US
(1 Pet. 2: 21–25)

Prepare for your lesson some little cards in the following manner:

Get a number of very small branches from a tree, and cut them up into short lengths, so that half of them will be two inches long, and the other half, three inches long. Make cards two by three inches in size. Fasten the little sticks on the cards in the shape of a cross. These can be fastened together on the card with a needle and thread. On the lower right-hand corner of the card write the reference 1 Pet. 2: 24. Prepare enough of these cards to give one to each pupil and a few extra ones that may be sent to the sick or shut-ins.

Write the subject of the lesson at the top of the blackboard. Have the pupils name things that Christ bore for us. Begin with the Babe in the manger, and go with them step by step through Christ's life; and, as the things He bore for us are named, have them written on the blackboard. Dwell on the last week of His life, the scene in the garden, His betrayal, His trial before Pilate, the journey from the prison to the cross, the crucifixion, the mocking, the casting lots for His garments, and the burial.

Try to impress on the class that Christ bore all of this for each one of us, that He bore it all to save us. Then lead the children to tell what we should do in return for this sacrifice and suffering.

VANITY FAIR

(1 John 2:15; Matt. 4:8-10)

You will need a balance for an object-lesson. You may be able to get one from your druggist or dentist. If you cannot, make it as follows:

The material will consist of some stiff pasteboard, a shallow pasteboard box, and some string. Cut the beam, standard, and pans out of the heavy pasteboard. The beam should be ten inches long and an inch wide at the centre, tapering to half an inch at the ends. The pans are square pieces of pasteboard; tie four cords, each five inches long, to the four corners of each square and fix the ends of the cords to the ends of the beam. Cut a narrow slit in the centre of the box, put the standard through, and fasten the centre of the beam to the top by putting a pin through and bending it at both ends.

Have one of the pupils read about Vanity Fair from "Pilgrim's Progress." The pupils will readily see that it means the world with its vanities and sin. Have another pupil tell about Faithful, and how he was burned at the stake.

Pass the slips of paper among the pupils, and ask each one to write on his slip some vanity or sin we should avoid. Have several already written out; put these in one pan of the balance; and let each be discussed by the pupils. Put in some black cards to represent sin, some red cards to represent murder, envy, etc.; also put in a stick to represent the stake at which Faithful was burned.

Have the pupils each lay his slip in the pan. In the other pan put a card on which these words have been written: "The chariot and horses which carried Faithful to the celestial gate." This will be more attractive if a chariot and horses are sketched on the card. It should be heavy enough to raise the opposite pan. A small weight may be attached to the back of the card for this purpose.

Close with the beautiful lesson contained in the Scripture text, of how Christ resisted all these things and came through the world pure and unspotted, and He is ready to help us conquer.

HEAVEN
(Rev. 21: 1-7)

After the reading of the lesson outline some open gates on the blackboard. This will help to fasten the attention of the pupils on the subject. Above the gates print or write the word "Heaven." Now ask each pupil to rise and tell what he wants most in all the world; what he would ask if he could have anything he might wish for. As each tells what he wants, write it on the blackboard. When all are through, ask the children to turn to 1 Cor. 2: 9, and read it in concert. Then, step by step, lead the children to see that the very best we can imagine will be as nothing when Jesus comes; that, even if we have many beautiful things in this world, there will be far more beautiful things in the New Jerusalem.

Draw a brace in front of the word "Heaven," and ask one of the pupils to read Rev. 21: 4. Ask the pupils if they ever knew any one that had never cried, that had never sorrowed or suffered pain. Then write in the brace, "No tears," "No sorrow," "No pain," "No crying," "No night." Ask the pupils to name other things that will not be found in heaven; also things that we shall have there, such as the water of life, the Lamb of God, a mansion, etc.

Lead the pupils to tell how we must live if we are going to be with Jesus when He comes, and enjoy the things He has prepared for those who are worthy.

Teach Rev. 21:7 for a memory verse.

What I Would Be

I would be true, for there are those who trust me;
I would be pure, for there are those who care;
I would be strong, for there is much to suffer;
I would be brave, for there is much to dare;

I would be friend of all — the foe, the friendless;
I would be giving and forget the gift;
I would be humble, for I know my weakness;
I would look up — and laugh — and love — and lift.

HOWARD ARNOLD WALTER

www.ingramcontent.com/pod-product-compliance
Lightning Source LLC
Chambersburg PA
CBHW031348040426
42444CB00005B/232